THE SUICIDE CLUB

'In thea sapienta:'
In tea there is great wisdom and discernment

A lifetime in tea

1st Edition - Printed November 2010
2nd Edition - Printed May 2011

CREDITS

Malinga H. Gunaratne
Handunugoda Estate
Tittagalla, Ahangama
Sri Lanka
Mobile : +94 (0) 773 290 999
Email : malinga@bellmail.lk

Published by Sri Serendipity Publishing House
www.sriserendipity.com
Managing Editor : Juliet Coombe
Editor : MarkThompson
Co-Editor : Fathima Razik
Photography : Juliet Coombe
Design : Kavinda Dhammika
Design House
(www.designhousetoday.com)
Printed by : Tharanjee Prints, Sri Lanka

To Hugette
You are unique and very
special to us

PREFACE

I have often visited Herman on his lowland tea estate at Handunugoda and, after walking around the property, have landed up on his verandah sipping a cup of fine Ceylon tea, to be regaled and enthralled with stories from his earlier tea planting days. I was thus delighted when, a few weeks ago, he told me that he had at last finished his tea memoirs and asked me whether I would write an introduction.

"A pleasure and an honour," I said. The following day a buff-coloured envelope arrived and I took out the manuscript to begin reading. Herman had emphatically told me that this was not an autobiography but a series of anecdotes and vignettes about his planting days, a distinction made equally clear by Gore Vidal in his work *Palimpsest*, where he wrote, 'A memoir is how one remembers one's own life, while an autobiography is history.'

The result is a wonderful collection of stories that brings alive not only all aspects of the plantation Raj's life which began with a morning gin and tonic and ended with an arrack and soda, but also lays bare the dedication and hard work of a planter, describing days that began at 6am, finished at 6pm and often went further into the night with extra estate duties.

In the days of the British-managed plantations, jobs were usually acquired by connection rather than through ability, but Herman's journey began in a very Dick Whittington-like way: 'With all my worldly possessions in one suitcase I was going in search of my dreams.' Through his own acumen, he rises through the rigid ranks of the tea hierarchy, from Creeper to Assistant to Superintendent, and while meandering through this maze, documents a fascinating story of plantation life: from the rigid and often pompous formality of the British Raj, the flirtatious approaches of the pluckers, and the summer holiday romances with planters' daughters, to the strict etiquette of planters' clubs and the gentlemanly code of settling one's debts.

These memoirs, however, are not just vignettes of what many consider to be the heydays of Ceylon; they also touch seriously on the ill-fated nationalisation of the estates and the perfidy of politicians in politicising the running of the plantations for their own political ends.

Herman's memoirs will provide an original, entertaining and perceptive insight into the soul of Ceylon, which is an essential prerequisite to understanding Sri Lanka as it is today.

Geoffrey Dobbs
Founder of the Galle Literary Festival
Taprobane Island

Romance is in the
up-country but
the action is in
the low-country.
This is my story...

"A rather racy and revelatory glimpse into the world of the tea planter! Herman's fast-paced, behind-the-scene stories tell more than most readers will ever have gleaned from other tea-related biographies."

- Jane Pettigrew - Former editor of Tea International

On 'The Suicide Club' "I found your book totally fascinating and now would like to see it all for real."

- Penny Munro -Traveller

"An excellent read that grabs you from start to finish. The human story of the Suicide Club makes me appreciate every sip of Ceylon tea, that much more."

- Lasantha David - Writer

"As one planter to another it was necessary for me to let you know that I enjoyed your book very much it gave historical background to the fantastic time I spent working in Sri Lanka. There is something very special about your island Herman…the people of Sri Lanka have a warmth and generosity that we have never found elsewhere."

- Michael John Thorp – Former planter

The book is a fascinating series of snapshots into the "tea world", produced by a very skilled raconteur. I can see why there is interest in filming it. Your tact and refusal to see things in black and white (British all good/bad; nationalism all good/bad) does you credit as does your discretion - although the latter only serves to whet one's appetite for more stories.

I am also enjoying your White Tea (lack of virgins' sweat notwithstanding) which I am sure is doing my insides no end of good.

- Philip Katz- Queens Counsel in the UK

IN A NUTSHELL

The name Ceylon has magic in it. It rolls off the tongue nicely. It conjures in your mind waving palm trees, sandy beaches, spices and precious stones. It was considered the jewel in the crown of the King Emperor's mighty British Empire. Sri Lanka is little known in the world of tea. It is Ceylon tea that captured the discerning palates of the world. It was the politicians who changed the name from Ceylon to Sri Lanka, ostensibly for astrological reasons. If that is indeed the case, it has not worked because everything started going wrong with the name change. For contextual reasons I will be referring to the island as Ceylon.

These stories are from the ringside of the great plantation drama that was played out in independent Ceylon. I was a principal player in the drama, having first worked for the British Sterling interests and then for the State, which went on to nationalise the plantations. It is a story of colonial and post-colonial Ceylon. The placid British Plantation Raj went through many convulsions and upheavals. The apparent prosperity of the plantations became the envy of those who were advocating nationalisation and re-distribution of land. The convenient whipping boy was the plantation sector. Political populism triumphed over conventional wisdom.

This is the tale of the bitter struggles, the joys and sorrows, the harrowing experiences in the quest of advancing upwards in the esoteric preserve of the white man. It is also a tale of how we lived and loved in a sphere that was controlled by the upper crust of British aristocracy.

The story is a personal one, where a man with very little formal education rose to the very apex of the plantation pyramid. The journey was not easy. It is not the conquest that I wish to write about but the quest, which is strewn with many pitfalls, humiliations and disappointments, but happily, no bitterness. I was treated fairly and justly, even when I fought the white man at the height of his power. My own countrymen would not have been so indulgent with me as the barometer of judgement was more the ability to be servile than to be competent. The servility and sycophancy demonstrated by the people of our country seem to endorse most comprehensively all the misdeeds of those holding powerful office!

All stories are true and if, in certain instances, I change some names around, it is because I do not want to embarrass the players in this drama.

As the stories unfold, I am hopeful that the reader will be able to capture the essence of life on the plantations. It is a story that can be written only if you have experienced life during the period of the British Raj.

It deals with the period of initiation. First appointments, tormenting dinners, an irreverent trout fisherman, and mischievous planters making untidy and unheard-of uses of the ladies' rest rooms at the planters' clubs, and of applicants for jobs offering to do 'nice nice' things to staid British planters' wives.

Twilight ladies, mischievous and sometimes provocative flirtations of the British girls who came to Ceylon for the summer holidays, wining and dining with King Emperor Mountbatten of

My mother Isla was humiliated and insulted by her own. She handled the white man with elegance.

Burma, Admiral of the Fleet, and dealing with the most powerful political leaders of our country - these were all a part of the varied experiences that I was privileged to have.

Special mention must be made of the Suicide Club. This was an informal association of the wealthiest men in Ceylon at that time. It was a gamblers club and my grandfather was the President. Enormous fortunes were won and lost at the sessions of the Suicide Club. Honour came before penury and gambling altered the fortunes of our entire family.

My education was interrupted due to the upheavals caused by the lack of funds. My grandfather's enormous wealth was lost due to gambling. My father Richard, too, gambled away a very valuable property a couple of miles away from Kandy. He received this as a dowry. He lost his own ancestral property, Mittrananda Estate in Sultanagoda, also on the roll of the dice.

The headquarters of the Suicide Club was 'Nalagiri' in Matara. It stands even today as a mute testimony to my grandfather, K. C. Albert De Silva.

Neither time nor the elements have affected this grand old mansion with tennis courts, driver's quarters and rolling lawns. Old residents of Matara say that, 'It is solid as the man who built it.' It is no more in the family. My uncle sold it for a pittance to a neighbour. It is still the most majestic house in Matara.

The book is also about dedication to duty and the hard life that a plantation manager had to endure to make a success of his chosen profession. I was taught life's lessons of how to deal with embarrassment and humiliation, not always at the hands of the British, but by my own people.

I was influenced to join the plantations by my father, who was an Area Manager of the Standard Vacuum Oil Company of America. Travelling up to Nuwara Eliya, Ceylon's hill country resort, he related wonderful stories of his roistering friends and classmates who were assistant managers of up-country plantations. 'They are paid in Sterling, they live in wonderful bungalows and they

take me to the club when I stay with them. We drink till morning but they have to be at Muster at 5am.' It is indeed strange that an innocent statement like that remained in my memory and influenced me to seek my fortune as a planter. I must have been 12 years old at that time.

It was a well-known and much talked-about fact that to join the plantations, one had to have important and well-placed connections. My family was not lacking in these highly placed, pompous, arrogant men. In fact we could have filled up a couple of rooms with these specimens! And even then, some would have been standing in the corridors! They represent the worst forms of the human condition!

My mother, an extremely attractive woman, went to meet a relative to seek his support on my behalf. This man was the epitome of arrogant pomposity. When my mother told him about my educational qualifications, he laughed in her face. He told her, 'Isla, just forget about it. Your son may not even be able to enter the plantations as a Conductor. It is impossible. I cannot help you.' He dismissed this hopeful woman with disdain. This was his brutal, cruel verdict. She came back and related this story to me.

As if to add salt to the wound he had boasted, 'Look at my son. He joined a leading commercial company in Colombo and was sent for overseas training. He now plays golf with his European boss.' To this pompous ass (for that is what he was), playing golf with the white man was the acme of achievement. His son was later sacked by his golfing colleague and I was, later on in my career, elevated to the position of Regional Manager of a 100,000 acres of Ceylon's best tea lands in Nuwara Eliya.

My humiliation began even before I started. An early lesson was learnt and I never, ever, went to anyone to 'put in a word for me.' Throughout a period spanning almost 45 years, I never solicited the support of any outsider in the advancement of my career. One was judged purely on one's ability and performance.

The only alternative available to me was to enter the

plantations as a trained man. My father had a friend, M. K. M. P. R. Rama Ramanathan Chettiar. He came from the reputed family of Nattukotai Chettiars, the first merchant bankers to the Ceylonese community.

Rama (as he was called) took me on as an unpaid creeper at his family estate, Narangalla Group, Aranayaka. Rama was the agent for the Standard Oil Company in Galle. To this day I bless him.

The stories will move forward from my stewardship at Narangalla Group. It will move across the rapidly changing landscape of the plantations in the various districts of Ceylon.

Yet another personal story is the contribution made by one woman, Hugette, a Parisienne with whom I shared the most tender of years. How she set an example to my two sons, Maithri and Vishva, who later went on to become lawyers. How she took charge of them and cared for them, and was the person who made the single most important contribution to my life and that of my two sons. How she bought a property in Puttalam, in the North Western area of Ceylon, to escape from me when I was insufferable. How she fled to Puttalam with my sons happily joining her, and leaving me alone to realise that I cannot always have it my way.

Of happy days spent in France in the 16th Arrondisement (Seizieme) where she lived with her daughter, of gambling in Monte Carlo and travelling there from her villa at Le Lavandou in the South of France, are all great memories. And most of all, the great confidence that she gave Maithri and Vishva at that time of their lives. 'Never be impressed by anyone. You are the best in the world. Remember, if misfortune ever befalls you wherever you are, and whatever you do, Poupy (that's what they called her) will be there for you. I know your father. He is a risk taker, in a way a gambler. His grandfather gambled with money. Your father will gamble with his life. He will never think of consequences, and you might have to walk out into the streets not knowing what to

do the next day. Whatever happens, I want you to promise that you will contact your Poupy.' My sons did not love me any less but they may have loved her a little more. More about her later.

The story deals with a plantation strike that threatened to spread through the length and breadth of the country. Of mercenaries hired to protect life and limb. Of British peers who advised my agents to give me a 'change of scenery,' a euphemism for a compulsory transfer. It is also the story of strong loyalties, against all odds, to stand by our superiors when they were in trouble. Of wining and dining with the Commander of the Navy at the British Naval Headquarters in Trincomalee (in the East), with the Naval Band playing lilting music for us while we drank the choicest of wines and partook of tender sirloin steaks!

I want the story to be one of guidance for the present day planting student. A lesson on how it was during the days of the British Plantation Raj.

This industry which was bequeathed to this country by the British is still the principal foreign exchange earner for the island. It is a sad indictment on our people that the crops are declining dramatically, tea factories are being shut down arbitrarily, and the entire organised plantation sector is in complete disarray. It brings to my mind a famous poem on Ceylon, described as an island:

> ***'Though every prospect pleases, And only man is vile'***

Malinga H. Gunaratne
Handunugoda Estate
Tittagalla
Ahangama

Portrait of K.C. Albert De Silva - my Grandfather - the President of The Suicide Club. "To lose everything that you have and walk away honourably was the hallmark of a Man"

Herman

THIS IS WHERE IT ALL BEGAN

NARANGALLA GROUP, ARANAYAKA

I went with hope and great determination to Narangalla Group, Aranayaka. This large plantation was situated in the Mawanella Electorate of the Kegalle District. It had belonged to Rama Ramanathan Chettiar's family for a number of years. They had bought it from the previous English owner, Mr. Lacey. Narangalla was planted in tea in the upper areas of the estate and rubber in the lower slopes.

I travelled up to the estate by bus from Colombo and hired a rickety old Vauxhall car to Narangalla. The car had seen better days, and it stalled several times on the way due to overheating. We had to stop and wait till the engine cooled and pour fresh cold water into the radiator. An inauspicious beginning, one would have thought. Not so with me. I was grimly determined to present myself to Rama, the Proprietor, with as much composure as I could muster.

I carried with me one suitcase containing all my worldly possessions which comprised just a few shirts, two pairs of pants, three pairs of shorts, a few planters' stockings and two pairs of stout, robust shoes. This was a meagre wardrobe when you compare it with what a creeper of today would carry for his first appointment. The austere wardrobe was all we could afford with the depletion of finances as a consequence of the Suicide Club!

I must however make it very clear to the reader that I admired my grandfather immensely and the activities of the Suicide Club did not diminish my reverence for him. I may even have secretly admired his reckless disdain for money. So, with my father.

I realised that it is not what you wear but the manner in which you wear it and the way you carry yourself that matters. I walked with confidence and dignity to take my first faltering steps to learn the rudiments of plantation work.

The road to Narangalla was long and winding. One had to pass the rubber section of the estate on the lower slopes to get to the Proprietor's bungalow. This bungalow was on the

highest elevation amidst a vast acreage of tea. It was like living in the high hills of the Himalayas. In retrospect, the tea plantation appeared to be not so lush and somewhat neglected. With the stops on the way, the journey took longer than anticipated.

I reported to the bungalow which was large and sprawling and commanded a panoramic view of the Mawanella valley. I walked in high anticipation to be met by my father's friend, Rama. He was a tall, distinguished Tamil gentleman who spoke impeccable English. He wore the traditional *verti* with a long white banian (vest).

"So, you are Richard's son," he said, extending a warm handshake. "Welcome to Narangalla. This is my family plantation and we run it with our own staff." By this he meant that the staff belonged to the Indian Chettiar Tamil community. He introduced me to the Head Clerk, Padmanabha who spoke only Tamil. He was also *verti*-clad. He did not seem too glad to have me around, and his reception was rather lukewarm. Usually sensitive to atmosphere, I ignored the cool reaction to my presence.

Various other officers were introduced to me. All of them were *verti*-clad with long banians and had the traditional holy ash rubbed on their foreheads. "This is Sinniah, the rubber maker. He will take you round and teach you how to do the work," Rama told me. I was taken aback. Here was I, coming to learn work on a tea plantation, being entrusted to a rubber maker! Sinniah was dark complexioned, had a huge stomach and wore a turban round his head. I will make the best of it, I thought to myself.

I was then taken to the room which I was to occupy during my stewardship on Narangalla. I had to share it with three or four others, all members of the staff. An old, rusty iron bed was allocated to me and I gingerly placed my belongings on a table in the room. There was no tablecloth, and instead the table was covered with old newspapers. The bed had a moth-eaten

mattress, supported on some wooden planks. This was where I was going to lay my tired bones to rest after the day's work was done. I have slept in worse places, I thought, and resolved to make the best use of it.

The bathroom was unique. The plush toilet seats had been removed, and there was clear evidence of the dismantling. Squatting pans had replaced the seats. The staff, who were all called Kanakapulles (KPs), preferred to squat than to sit on a low level suite!

Since it was now time for lunch, I was ushered into a community dining room. The lunch comprised *thosai* and some *sambol* served on silver plates. I then realised that my initiation into the world of the British Plantation Raj was going to be on a vegetarian Indian diet of *thosai* (a thin pancake made out of flour) and *idli* (a blob of a flour cake, which I could somehow not eat, however hungry I was).

The food was served by a cook who did not bother about what and how much of the *thosai* or the curry I wanted on my plate. He just walked around dumping his preparations onto my plate with a silver ladle. You have to stoop to conquer, I thought to myself, swallowing the *idli* with large doses of water in order not to offend my hosts.

I was totally unaccustomed to this lifestyle of community living on a vegetarian diet. All this I could cope with, but the loud and happy belching after the meals took a little time to get used to. The unusual noises continued. I got used to it.

After the *thosai* and *idli* diet, Sinniah the Rubber Maker invited me to visit the tea fields with him and introduced me to Mr. B. A. Fernando, the Superintendent of the estate. Mr. Fernando was the only other Sinhalese on the property. He was a genial man of about 45 years of age. He was always smiling and extended to me a very warm and hearty welcome. Though he was the Superintendent I soon realised that he did not have much authority on the plantation. He was dressed in khaki shorts of the early Christian variety, coming down well below

his knees. He wore a large pith hat on his head. Not the picture of sartorial elegance.

Mr. Fernando and Sinniah were great friends. Sinniah was my first teacher and what a wonderful man he was. He taught me the elementary principles of plucking, pruning, weeding and manuring, and labour management. He told me wonderful stories of the British planters who worked on Narangalla. Sinniah spoke Sinhala reasonably well but quickly told me that he would soon speak to me only in Tamil. His role model of a planter was Mr. Lacey, the previous owner. He constantly referred to Lacey *Dorai* (Master).

We ended our first field round on my first day on the plantations at around 6pm. Sinniah told me very clearly that I had to be ready for morning Muster at 6am and wanted me to report to the Muster shed from where he was to take me on a more comprehensive tour of the estate. He repeated that from the next day he would talk to me only in Tamil.

I retired to the bungalow happily tired and longing for a bath, having travelled all the way from Colombo on this, my first day. The evenings in Narangalla were very cold. The elevation was around 3000 feet above sea level. I thought I would be able to have a hot water bath but it was not to be. The Kanakapulles had removed the hot water system and preferred to boil the water in big barrels and pour it over their heads with a small bowl, one pouring the water over the other, and then reversing the process. I realised that no one was going to boil water for me, least of all pour it over my tired body. Bath time was clearly a period of fun and frolic for the Chettiars. They were slapping each other on the back and soaping each other's bodies rhythmically and with loud guffaws.

I watched this community bathing episode with interest. The laughter was infectious and the tension of the moment and the unknown was lightened. I slowly crept into the toilet and looked for what remained of an old shower. There was one, without a shower head. By this time I was prepared to

All my worldly
belongings...

jump into the cold Antarctic Ocean just for the luxury of a bath. I opened the tap of the shower hoping that water would come gushing through the pipe. It did. The water was ice cold coming all the way from a natural spring higher up on the mountain. I was now making a virtue out of necessity and convinced myself that an ice cold water bath was good for my health! As indeed it was.

It was now dinner time. More *thosai* and more *wade´* (a spicy preparation of dhal, chillies and onions) with a different *sambol*. I thanked all the angels that there was no *idli* left because I could not take any more of it, as it felt like it was coming out of my ears. I enjoyed this frugal vegetarian meal to the loud accompaniment of more burping and belching from my fellow diners. They had loud discussions in Tamil while dining. I did not understand a word of what they said. I resolved to learn Tamil as quickly as possible.

It was now time to retire for a good night's sleep. I crept into my iron bed with a hard wooden head and took stock of my first day in the Plantation Raj. Changing into a *sarong* (a loose comfortable cloth tied deftly round the waist) had to be done in the open with my roommate curiously watching my preparations for sleep. My fellow colleagues, however, were talking deep into the silent night and smoking a special type of Jaffna cigar which certainly did not possess the fragrant aroma of its Cuban counterpart!

I had arrived on the path to fulfilling my ambition. My unusual companions and the loud noises did not deter me from a good night's sleep. My mind was focused on learning the basics of plantation management. I looked forward to the dawn of the new day.

I carried a little note book in which I wrote down all the Tamil words necessary to make even a very rudimentary conversation. I knew that if I achieved mastery over the language, I would be accepted into the club. This was indeed the best thing that happened to me. I was thrown into the deep end and I had to learn to swim!

The next day dawned with the mist rolling up to the bungalow from the valley below. The sight was inspiring and I was reminded of the Himalayas about which I had read in school.

I walked to the Muster ground before anyone else appeared and waited with some excitement for my first full day as a Creeper. Sinniah was the next to arrive followed by Mr. Fernando, who came to Muster smoking the same type of Jaffna cigar as my other sleeping companions. Then came the pluckers, the pruners and an assorted lot of sundry workers - all gazing at this new 'specimen' on their estate. With whatever dignity I could muster I stood erect and tried to look confident. I received positive vibrations from the workers and the other members of the minor staff.

The Tamil plucking ladies were colourfully attired in resplendent, gaily-coloured sarees. The younger ones stole bashful glances at this new creeper! They all carried cane plucking baskets and a coarse blanket that was called a *cumbly*. This was to protect them from the extreme cold weather and the rain. Some of them were pretty and flirtatious. They whispered to each other, stealing careful glances at me. I stood upright and very proper, although not unmindful of their attraction and smiles. Many a young British planter had fallen victim to this fatal attraction and were sent back home to England unceremoniously!

One young woman, Rajaletchimi, was the prettiest of them all. She was not shy and was a very good plucker, always bringing high poundage. Like all pretty women in the world, she was aware of her good looks. I did not know it then, but she looked at me and muttered something to Sinniah. 'I am a good plucker and I will teach the young master how to pluck.' Sinniah told her to mind her own business and that he would look after my training. This was all good-humoured banter, and was usual at morning Muster.

Muster was quickly dispersed and the workers were allotted

Narangalla 50 years on is
no longer a tea plantation.
The closed factory has
become a shed to hang
washing in, and the big
bungalow has a hole in the
wall. The sky is the roof
and the jungle has taken
over...

different duties. The muster chit was marked to be sent to the Proprietor and Sinniah took me on my first field round.

Sinniah spoke Sinhala and English reasonably well. He told me that he learnt his English from Lacey *Dorai*. His first lesson was that, 'Master must not get too friendly with the pluckers,' sensing the stolen glances exchanged between the pluckers and myself.

He then took me to the plucking field. He told me that the most important job on a plantation was plucking. "He who masters plucking masters the estate," he said. These words echo through my mind to this day. He taught me the intricacies of plucking and insisted, straightaway, that I wear a basket on my head and started plucking. I was told that a plucker brings 30 pounds a day and in order to supervise them properly I had to do the same. I readily consented to do this. He allocated an old seasoned plucker to be at my side and supervise my work. He placed me as far away from Rajaletchimi as possible!

He left me in the plucking field and continued to supervise other areas. There was some deference when he spoke to me and I realised that there was acceptance that I may, eventually, make the grade. I continued harvesting the two leaves and the bud in silence. The old plucker kept a watchful eye on me and told me what to pluck and what to leave on the bush. It was hard work initially but I persisted. There were twitters and sly glances from the younger ones, chatting gaily in Tamil. I knew they were casting remarks about the newcomer, not in an unfriendly way, but in fun. This went on for about two hours and I could hardly collect two pounds, when the ladies around me were all filling their baskets with green leaf, their nimble finger flitting fast over the tea bushes. I was going to fight all the way and match up to them. By sign language and guidance, the old plucker trained me and I picked up fast. Interest is the secret of success, I realised. Rajaletchimi came to me during the tea break and offered me some green leaf to swell my harvest in the eyes of Sinniah. The old woman, my trainer, chased her away.

Sinniah came back to the plucking field about three hours later, inspected my basket, spoke to my teacher and finally acknowledged that I was not a bad pupil. He spoke in rapid Tamil to the trainer who I think told him that the new *Dorai* was a serious guy. This I could glean from the body language and the smiles of the others after Sinniah spoke to my teacher. Sinniah felt a little sorry for me and said, 'that was enough for the day,' and that he wanted me to accompany him to the other work fields. I asked him if I could remain in the plucking field, not so much to impress him, but to gain mastery over plucking. He insisted that I stop, and come with him.

I could sense the recognition and being accepted as a good potential planter. Tamil was not too difficult to learn and I was progressing well. I am usually good at languages. Sinniah, my mentor, was enthused by my keenness and interest in my work, and I could sense that he was going to teach me all that he knew. He asked me about my family and how I came to know the Proprietor, Ramanathan Chettiar. To all the questions I gave honest answers and we were soon to establish a very easy relationship. Sinniah and I sat on a rock and had a cup of tea, after which he took out a Jaffna cigar and started puffing contentedly. I asked him if I could smoke a cigarette and he, not too surprised, told me to go right ahead. He was kind, genial and shrewd. He realised that I had come to Narangalla only for training and that I was not a threat to anyone.

He told me that he was going to be very hard on me and that he had the highest hopes that one day I would be a source of pride to him. We visited the other work fields and went back to the bungalow for a lunch of string hoppers and coconut sambol. This was a veritable feast for me. I loved string hoppers as passionately as I hated *idli*! There was no steak and kidney pie for me, however. The more fortunate planting students, who were lucky enough to join the agency house plantations dined on roast beef and potatoes, Yorkshire puddings and shepherd's pie. It was string hoppers for me.

This was the general routine. One day with Sinniah and the next with Mr. Fernando. I was slowly gaining acceptance. I knew Rama, the Proprietor, was obtaining confidential reports on my progress and seemed highly satisfied. The Chettiars, my roommates, were marvelling at my mastery of the Tamil language. This compulsory total absorption into Tamil speaking helped me in later life. At the examination of the Tamil language held by the Ceylon Planters' Society, I was the only Sinhalese candidate who got 98 marks out of 100 in spoken Tamil, thanks to Narangalla Group!

As is usual on these occasions, the Chettiars were asking various questions from me, to which I had to reply in Tamil. They also taught, before I gained a fair knowledge of the language, some phrases like, 'Come to me, you are beautiful, you have a big bottom,' claiming of course, that these words referred to some intricate aspect of plucking. The next day I uttered these words after practising the previous night. The pluckers broke out into peals of laughter. Sinniah looked at me in horror. "Who taught you to say that?" he asked angrily. When I replied that it was the Chettiars, he smiled, realising that the old men were having fun at my expense. "You are not to learn any more Tamil from them," he admonished me.

Life was not exciting because of the mundane routine. One day was pretty much like the next. However, it was interesting for me because I loved the job and was totally immersed in the learning process. I was now longing for some company where I could not only speak in English but also associate with aspiring planters. Narangalla was far removed from the Plantation Raj that I was aspiring to join!

It was at about this time that there was a pleasant surprise on Narangalla. Two beautiful young ladies arrived in this all-male plantation domain. The Proprietor's daughters, Margaret and Rosemarie. Both convent-educated, accomplished and very friendly. The atmosphere at the big bungalow softened with the arrival of these two girls. They, like me, may have found the Chettiars a little too awkward for their polished, convent-educated ways.

Margaret was a tall, dark and pretty girl. She wore a short flared skirt which did justice to her shapely legs. The T-shirts that she wore did not hide her quite ample bosom. She was around 16 to 17 years old. We established a very formal relationship, starting with the usual 'Good Morning' and 'Good Night.' They spoke impeccable English. The Chettiars spoke no English at all. We could therefore advance from greetings to more personal topics with no one being the wiser! For two months I had forgotten what a chocolate tasted like. Margaret slowly slipped these delicacies to me when no one was watching. I ate them only when I was out on the field. These Cadbury chocolates with the different flavoured soft centres came from an unlimited stock that Margaret seemed to produce on a daily basis. I had to eat them surreptitiously without the Chettiars ever knowing about these gifts. The Chettiars knew no English but they could read and understand the language of the eyes. I knew that this was leading to a closer association which may have brought my apprenticeship to an abrupt end. I was cautious, although Margaret was not. She found every excuse to speak to me. She was the Proprietor's daughter, and I was the Creeper, desperately looking for a job. I knew eventually that the daughter of the King could do no wrong!

English tuition was the most convenient way. I, who had not even passed my eighth standard, ended up giving tuition to both Margaret and Rosemarie. The Chettiars were watching these teaching sessions with some suspicion, but the lessons were conducted right out in the open and therefore they could do nothing about it. Rama, too, saw the daughters adding new words to their vocabulary and was not too unhappy about the tuition classes.

A gentle caress when passing a book, her feet softly caressing mine under the table, were the signals that Margaret gave me about the possibility of a more intimate relationship. I reciprocated without reluctance. I was not made of stone! She wrote little notes to me, in the guise of giving me essays for correction. The essays were one page, the notes were two pages.

However, Padmanabha, the trusted man of the Proprietor, gently warned me, "These are young girls, you must be careful!" Rama, too, was casting watchful glances when the girls were talking to me and the lessons were abruptly suspended.

By this time, I was entrusted with the total responsibility of looking after some tea fields. This job, I knew, I had done exceptionally well. It was easy to compare my areas with those supervised by the others. Rama himself came to the field to see my work. I was useful to the estate. The crops were increasing, the fields were looking good. I was not kicked out

of Narangalla. The daughters went back to the convent ahead of schedule. Rosemarie was not too happy with the attention that Margaret was receiving from me and was vying with her sister for my attention. Margaret promised to stay in touch and write to me. I was not keen on exchanging letters as I knew that they may get into the wrong hands. The farewells were subdued and tender.

I had, now, a new status on the estate. The Chettiars knew the Proprietor's daughters were a little too fond of me and that the Proprietor himself did not totally disapprove of the association. I will always remember Margaret and Rosemarie, who lightened my drab and humdrum existence with their gentle presence. I have often wondered where fate and destiny took these two lovely girls. I received one letter from Margaret which, reluctantly, I did not reply. I thought it better not to.

One day led to another. I was gaining mastery over the Tamil language and plantation work. This was recognised by all those on Narangalla. It was not difficult for me to command the respect of the labour as I could do everything I asked them to do just as well. I was, however, no nearer my goal of joining the Plantation Raj.

It was on one of these days that I had a rather fortuitous meeting. I was supervising the plucking on a roadside field on Narangalla when I chanced upon two well-dressed young planters travelling down the road. Normally these planters from the bigger estates did not break bread with those like me, who were on what was derogatorily called a 'native estate.' They stopped and greeted me, I think out of curiosity.

They introduced themselves to me. "I am Cubby Wijetunga and this is Shelly Ryde. We are both from Glenalmond Estate next door," said Cubby, the senior of the two. Cubby was a tall, well-built guy with a cherubic face, bespectacled and kindly. Shelly was an extremely handsome man, and both were very smartly dressed in serge shorts and well-tailored, expensive shirts. They were shod in well-polished brown shoes with smart stockings. This was in complete contrast to my well-worn khaki shorts and simple checked shirt. My shoes were in need of extensive repair.

Never feeling inferior in any given situation I told them that I was 'creeping' on Narangalla. "Which school did you go to?" asked Cubby. "St. Thomas' College, Mount Lavinia," I replied. I knew full well that this would establish me as a peer. We had a long chat and Cubby told me that he was the Assistant Superintendent of Glenalmond and that Shelly was also creeping on the property. He also told me that there was another Creeper, whose name was Tony.

Cubby was a sensitive guy. He realised that I was living in unusual surroundings with hardly any company. He said "We must all get together. You must come to dinner to my bungalow soon." Never one to take up invitations given as a mere courtesy, I was grateful but did not accept with alacrity.

Days passed uneventfully, when Cubby sent a message through a worker asking me to come to dinner on a particular day. I was happy to respond. I wore my best pair of pants with a well pressed shirt and presented myself at the Glenalmond Assistant Superintendent's bungalow. Cubby and Shelly greeted me with great warmth and introduced me to the other Creeper, Tony. We had a long night chatting gaily away, drinking Old Arrack, and recounting each other's experiences. I regaled them with stories of the Chettiars and my life on Narangalla. I was now in far more comfortable surroundings with proper toilets and hot water on tap, an extreme luxury for me. We spoke about our hopes and aspirations. Shelly, Tony and I were of the same status, albeit from different situations. Cubby, I think, had sympathy for the conditions under which I was learning work. He was my friend, guide and advisor. He was gentle enough, however, never too overbearing or overly sympathetic. I hated sympathy. After some time, all three of them could not do without me. I was regularly taken to Glenalmond, fed and looked after as one of their own.

Munidasa was Cubby's cook and 'Man Friday.' It was with Cubby and the others that I had an opportunity of tasting roast chicken, roast beef and the inevitable caramel pudding after about three months on a strict vegetarian diet. Cubby even asked me, "Why don't you live with us and go to Narangalla for work?" This was trespassing on their kindness too much and I declined. It made little difference, though, because most of the time I was on Glenalmond. He introduced me to his Manager, Harold Winter, who was considered a tyrant. Harold and I got on like a house on fire. He, too, taught me the finer points of plantation management.

Cubby was capable of bigger things and was also looking for employment in the British-owned and managed plantations. Glenalmond was a good launching pad. It belonged to a group of plantations owned by Harris de Kretzer. Kretzer and Winter's recommendations were recognised by the plantation companies. Cubby then gently told me that I should endeavour to obtain training from a more recognised company. He said to me, "Join a place like Galamuduna Group for six months, get a certificate and then apply for a job. You will get it."

He further obtained Harold Winter's permission for me to spend a few days with him on Glenalmond under his tutelage. I realised that there was far more to learn from Cubby and agreed to this brief period on Glenalmond. I periodically went round the fields with him. Glenalmond had a large population of village labour coming to work from a place called Getaberiyakanda. It was here that I saw the most beautiful women in my life. There was a Kangany called Rankira who had the three most beautiful daughters. One was Seetha. She is still, after so many years, the most provocatively innocent and pretty girl that I have ever seen. Seetha had the complexion of a king coconut. Rounded breasts, with lips like rosebuds, tall and elegant, with a musical voice and she was a good plucker to boot.

One of us fell hopelessly in love with Seetha. We got to

the field at noon just to watch her bringing the day's harvest to the factory. With the basket balanced on her head and her buttocks rolling with her innocently provocative walk, she was indeed a sight to behold. We advised the love struck friend that this could not go on for the sake of our careers which were nowhere near our chosen goals. An association with Seetha was going to result in the early termination of a very promising future on the plantations. Seetha was the ultimate coquette, flashing her eyes, rolling her behind, bending forward in my friend's presence so that her rounded breasts could be seen ever so slightly. She became just an obsession and nothing more.

I took Cubby's advice to join Galamuduna Group, Dolosbage. We were all young men in search of our dreams and aspirations. I wrote to my father to see if he could obtain for me a 'creeping' period on Galamuduna Estate, which belonged to the Panadura Tea and Rubber Company. This company was owned by some very close relatives.

I mentioned to Cubby that I had taken steps to carry out his advice and was getting positive signals of being taken in by Galamuduna, not as a paid creeper but as one who had to pay the estate for the privilege of learning work. The letter finally arrived and I was preparing to leave my abode at Narangalla. Cubby wanted to give me a farewell party and we decided to go for the Railway Dance at Nawalapitiya. This was going to be my farewell.

Shelly Ryde was sending us wild with his descriptions of the Burgher girls at the Railway Quarters in Nawalapitiya. Shelly, himself from the Burgher community, knew them all. He gave all of us, starved of female company, some very encouraging news that he would find partners for us. He enthralled us with titillating descriptions of his cousin, Judy. Her contours, her charm and beauty were described to us in great detail. We made careful preparations for the Railway Dance. The big question was, who was going to partner Judy?

Cubby Wijetunga was in charge. He was the first among equals. He had an extensive wardrobe and, after all, he was the only person getting a salary. Shelly and Tony, not to be outdone, had their own glad rags. I was rather lacking in this department but although I didn't have the clothes I had confidence in ample measure.

Cubby had a very expensive Copacabana shirt which was the envy of us all. He also had a well cut suit. Shelly and Tony had cocktail attire of pants in one colour and coat in another. I had no coat, no tie and my shoes were more suitable to kick stones in the tea fields than to do the Foxtrot or the Viennese Waltz! I told them, "Don't worry, I will brazen it out, saying that Nawalapitiya is too warm to wear a coat." Cubby knew I could handle this. He always had confidence in my ability to talk my way out of a situation.

Meticulous planning was required. We were to walk 10 miles from the Kegalle district to the Nawalapitya electorate in the Kandy district. The Railway Dance was to be held at the Railway Sports Club. Ten miles for a dance. It was almost like the story of the pioneer planters!

We pooled our resources. Cubby was the banker. We had not only to buy the tickets for ourselves but also for our partners. This was too much for Cubby.

"What time does the dance start?" he asked Shelly.

"8pm," was the reply.

"Here's what we do," said Cubby, like a General Officer mapping out a battle plan. "We arrive late to the dance. By this time our partners tickets will have been bought by their parents. We apologise profusely, saying that we were delayed because of a hold up with labour pay. I will make a feeble attempt to pay the ticket fees, and let's hope like hell that they refuse."

He then told me, "You, Herman, chip in at this stage and say that all the drinks will be on us for the rest of the evening. There will already be drinks and bottles on the table as the

Railway guys are not going to start a dance without a few shots. So you don't have to worry too much. You walk out to the bar but slip into the changing rooms where we will have a few bottles of arrack hidden in our suitcases. You come back and place a bottle with a flourish on the table, and this will buy us some respectability and a respite for some time."

Cubby went on, "Don't drink from our bottle, drink from theirs. Walk around, there are bound to be fellow, well-heeled planters, all trying to impress the Railway girls. They will offer you drinks, so go for it in large doses," instructed Cubby. This all sounded terribly interesting and was creatively thought out. It is perhaps the same creative thinking that propelled Cubby to the highest position of Chairman of Nestlé, one of Ceylon's leading multi-national companies! All these moves would be executed with panache and elegance.

Shelly then made the introductions to our respective partners, all lovely charming girls, but Judy, she was something special

- tall, fair skinned, with lovely flowing hair, although it was her legs that stole the show. A short flared red skirt ballooning out with buckram borders, was in vogue at the time. It was as if these skirts were made not so much to conceal as to reveal lovely legs, well proportioned and not an ounce of flesh out of place, almost taunting the other girls to come up with better legs. Judy was the jewel of the night. And we were handing her over on a plate to Cubby!

Cubby was going to partner Judy. This was only befitting as he was our leader and there had to be some reciprocation for his expansive kindness. We were questioning Shelly, "Has she got any sisters like her, can't you find another like her for us?" There was only one Judy that night. Just to elevate Cubby in the eyes of the girls, we started calling him 'Sir' and Cubby grandly told us, "Come on boys, we are not on the estate any more, you don't have to be formal here." Just the same, we established his supremacy and our position as his assistants.

Cubby stood tall that night, but the dance was still not over. It had only started. There were more surprises to come.

Shelly and Tony were good dancers. I was the clumsy fellow. Dancing never appealed to me. I would rather stand at the bar and have a good conversation. We all took to the dance floor and managed to dance through a few slow numbers. Cubby was watching the passing scene with a glint in his eye. He was not dancing. The level of our host's bottles was sinking fast. This is when Cubby made the move.

He beckoned me casually and told me almost in a whisper, "Can you do me a favour? Walk up to the band, and give the leader a four finger shot of arrack. Then ask him to carry on with the same music and suddenly switch on to the Blue Danube waltz, and continue thereafter with a few more waltzes." I did not know one waltz from another and asked Cubby what on earth he was trying to do. "You get it done," was all he said.

I walked casually up to the leader, introduced myself as the Assistant Superintendent of Glenalmond Estate, which, by the way, I was not, and placed the glass in his hand. He gulped it down with gusto. "My boss over there," I said, "wants to offer you a special gift if you can suddenly switch on to a couple of waltzes." Having tasted our unsolicited generosity, he agreed.

I gave Cubby the thumbs up sign. He took to the floor with Judy. This is when I saw the real Cubby. He danced like a swan. It soon became obvious that he was the best dancer on the floor, but more was to come. The band leader looked at me, I nodded my head and then he started on a waltz.

There were howls of protest. Few of those present could dance the waltz. But Cubby and Judy kept the crowd enthralled with a session of the most elegant dancing I have ever seen. He glided across the floor, guiding Judy delicately through the complicated steps of the Blue Danube and the other Viennese waltzes, and it was a display of such brilliant elegance that the atmosphere became electric. Everybody left

the floor. Cubby and Judy were now the cynosure of all eyes. He varied the steps, he twirled Judy round on his finger. He spun on his heels. He turned Judy round on her heels. It was truly a performance of a master. The crowd slowly realised what was happening and were watching this accomplished display with open-mouthed awe. Then they involuntarily broke into applause. Cubby and Judy received a standing ovation. Our night was made.

We dined and drank that night on Cubby's reflected glory. We switched over to whisky and brandy, since everybody was eager to offer us drinks. We kept knocking them down. By this time, everyone was nine sheets to the wind, having a good time without a care in the world. I grabbed somebody else's bottle and gave it not only to the band leader but to the entire band. The promised gift was delivered. Someone else paid for it.

We had walked to Nawalapitiya and swept the Railway community off their feet. The next day was a Sunday and we had several invitations to lunch. Our hosts, Judy's parents, were proud of us. The issue of the tickets was forgotten. We had come for the dance with barely a nickel or a dime and walked away with the show.

Judy faded out of our lives but not before Shelly and I paid a visit to her uncle's house in Dehiwala, a suburb of Colombo, and invited her for another dance. She was leading a cloistered life with her wealthy guardian uncle and could not make it, or thought it better not to.

That was my farewell to Narangalla, from Cubby, Shelly and Tony.

I walked into Galamuduna not
as a completely uninitiated
novice, but with a good
knowledge of how
a plantation
functioned

MOVING FALTERINGLY FORWARD

GALAMUDUNA GROUP, DOLOSBAGE

With the passion for tea fired up after my short stint at Narangalla, I walked into Galamuduna not as a completely uninitiated novice, but with a good knowledge of how a plantation functioned. Knowledge was the secret to confidence.

Galamuduna was not far from Glenalmond or Narangalla. This 2000 acre plantation was situated on the western side of the Aranayaka range of hills. It comprised four or five divisions (a division was a distinct area of around 300-400 acres).

To understand the story better, it is important to outline the plantation hierarchy. The plantation structure established by the British was the most effective management system. It has stood the test of time. The overall chief of the plantation was the Manager or the Superintendent (PD meaning *Periya Dorai* in Tamil, or 'Big Master.') The second-in-command was called the Senior Assistant Superintendent, thereafter it was the Assistant Superintendents (SD, meaning *Sinna Dorai* in Tamil, or 'Small Master.') The 'Creeper' was an aspiring Assistant Superintendent, the lowliest 'specimen' on the plantation.

Every area on the plantation was under the purview of an officer designated for the purpose. The Manager and the Assistant, however, were in overall charge of every department. This delegation of authority and responsibility was at the will and pleasure of the 'King.'

The Manager, or the Superintendent, was King. The whole plantation revolved round him. He was the judge, juror and the dispenser of justice. The Assistant was the 'Prince' in charge of his designated division. This was the clearly established line of control.

The Manager set the tone for the running of the plantation. He was aloof from the rest of the staff. His abode and the dwellings of the Assistants were called bungalows. The staff lived in 'quarters' and the labour lived in 'lines.' Even the dwellings of those on the plantations had very distinct class stratifications!

Every problem on the plantation, including inter-family

squabbles, marital infidelity, thefts, births and deaths, was referred to the Manager for a final decision. Even a coffin was given free of charge to bury the dead. The Manager's decision was final. It was an extremely feudal system. The feudal overlord had to dispense justice without fear or favour. The estate was like a miniature government.

There was a well stocked grocery shop, a barber salon and even a well-stocked arrack tavern. We did not have to visit the hair dressing salon to get a haircut. The barber was simply summoned to the bungalow. The plantation was completely self-contained and we could live this way without any association or connection with the outside world. Some of us eventually began to think that the Estate was indeed the world!

The Manager of Galamuduna was Aelian De Silva. He was the most kindly and genial man one could find. He tried, not always successfully, to demonstrate a strict and aloof disposition. He spoke only a few words and those, too, only when absolutely necessary. Never too friendly during working hours, Aelian was a great planter. He was thorough with every aspect of the plantation management.

The first question when the assistants met on any given day was, 'How is the Old Man's mood today?' This was quickly communicated to all the other assistants. The mood of the 'Old Man' was assessed within minutes of meeting him in the morning.

Aelian started his day at 6am, every day. We were all out on the field 15 minutes before him. If he said 'Good morning' to you, the mood was not too bad, but if he waited for you to greet him first, he was not in top form, and one had to be careful till his mood changed for the better. The task of softening him up usually fell upon me because I met him before anyone else. I had mastered the art of getting him in the correct mood. This I did by greeting him first, respectfully, with a wide optimistic smile. It is difficult to be taciturn when someone is infectiously enthusiastic!

Aelian took charge of teaching me the finer points of plantation life. His bungalow was right on top of the hill, commanding a full view of the main plantation. His wife was the gentle and charming Nalini. She was the unobtrusive Eastern wife. Well-mannered, soft-spoken, she ran an immaculate bungalow. The bungalow was large, elegant and sprawling, with manicured lawns and an asphalt tennis court on the western side.

I was allocated a very comfortable room with an attached bathroom. A welcome change for me from the days of community living on Narangalla! Hot water was on tap. The *appu* (butler/chef) was dressed in immaculate white, with a tightly wrapped turban on his bald head. There was a string of minor domestic staff, cleaning the house and polishing the brass and silver. The floors were also polished daily. The big bungalow was spic and span. To me, this was the first real glimpse of how the planters lived.

My breakfast was served in my room. I had all the other meals with Aelian and his wife. Dinner was always a formal affair. Nalini dressed in a lovely saree and both of us men in smart casual attire. Aelian sat to dinner after two or three whiskies, while I watched this with my tongue hanging out!

It was invariably a two-or three-course meal with hot bread rolls and a delicious dessert.

Aelian loosened up at dinner and we discussed many matters concerning the plantation, politics and the neighbours, and made plans for the next day. Both of them were very fond of me, and I of them. I was to disappoint Aelian and Nalini, but that was later.

He questioned me closely on my progress and I knew that he was quite satisfied with the way I was shaping up. I was eager to learn, worked very hard and was a keen and willing Creeper. He allocated tasks to me from time to time. I made sure that all tasks given were accomplished to his entire satisfaction.

Galamuduna was in one of the highest rainfall areas in the

island, Dolosbage. It rained incessantly the whole day with no respite. On many occasions we did not see the sun for several days. The workers reported for work despite these conditions. They were drenched to the bone from early morning, as the day began. I can think of no human being who would work so cheerfully under these most unfavourable conditions as the Tamil plantation worker. The Sinhalese workers who came from the village, would simply absent themselves when it rained. It is to this Tamil worker that the country owes its biggest debt of gratitude. Without them the plantations just could not function. We who supervised them had to lead by example.

When it rained and they got wet, we too suffered the same fate. Some planters today carry an umbrella during the rains. To be under the shade of an umbrella when your workers are getting drenched is hardly leading by example. I never carried an umbrella. We had to wait till the lunch break to get into dry clothes which lasted only a few minutes in that comfortable condition before getting drenched once again. I was not told by anyone not to carry an umbrella. I just felt it was right not to do so. In later life on the plantations I insisted that my assistants, too, suffered the same fate as the pluckers. They could wear a waterproof jerkin, a waterproof hat, even waterproof pants, but they could not carry an umbrella. When the pluckers realised that the boss, too, was getting wet just as they did, there was greater respect and they worked harder. In the end this is what management is all about. You led by example.

Aelian entertained lavishly. I was asked to all the parties. When British planters visited the bungalow we were a little more formal in our attire. I rather suspected that Aelian was proud of his Creeper. I have seen many a Ceylonese planter tongue tied and nervous in the presence of Europeans. I had no such problem. The final act of acceptance was when they invited Aelian and Nalini for reciprocal parties, always asking them to bring me along.

When I visited their bungalows I closely studied the way the planters lived. The immaculate bungalows, the liveried staff, the almost clinical cleanliness within left a lasting impression on me. They were all polite and never left me out of the conversation. The discussions were never lively, they were non-controversial. It was small talk, and pretty mundane stuff about bungalows, lawns and gardens and the usual discussions about the difficulty in obtaining trained staff. Rather dull and in no way enlightening. I would much rather have stayed at home and read a book. I realised, however, that this was an essential part of the training as a planter, and went out of my way to be an eager participant at the discussions. I thought then that an Englishman was comfortable only when he was uncomfortable! I have changed my mind since as I have met some very lively and intelligent Englishmen.

These evenings were not entirely wasted. I learnt how to use the array of 'weapons' on an Englishman's dinner table. I learnt about morning rooms, smoking rooms and the polite expression of delight and appreciation at awfully bland food! All very prim and proper and sometimes so awfully hypocritical! Cubby's beef curry and a good coconut *sambol* for me any day!

Aelian and Nalini visited other planters and stayed over with them at the weekends. I was invited to join them. These visits, again, gave me an insight into how the others lived and worked. It also gave me a new status on the plantation as a guy who was very friendly with the Manager. Messages to be conveyed to Aelian were whispered to me, to be mentioned to him when the opportunity was ripe. This I did, ensuring always that I looked after the best interests of the other assistants. Never once did I carry any tales. All this contributed to a very harmonious atmosphere. I gradually realised that though I was only a Creeper, I had a rather elevated status on the property. During these visits I learnt much because most of those whom we visited were Aelian's Creepers in the past. They consulted him on the problems they had and Aelian always gave them very good advice. These discussions centred round how to handle Visiting Agents (VAs) who were the representatives of the owners and the agents who ran the plantations.

The days on Galamuduna were not without moments of high fun. One day, the Manager of Mossville Estate, Sanka Moonesinghe, had organised a party at the bungalow of the owner of both Mossville and Malgolle estates. The party was at Malgolle Estate. The owner was Mrs. Charles P. Laing. She was away on holiday in the UK. The bungalow was the last word in elegance, much like a small British castle. Well appointed lawns, a large swimming pool, racing stables and billiards rooms were all a part of Malgolle.

The Laings had a string of thoroughbred race horses. Stanley Perera, the Assistant Superintendent, was tasked with looking after the animals. He also had to present Mrs. Laing with flowers every week. This was the subject of many a jest at Stanley's expense. 'You give her flowers. What does she give you?' Mrs. Laing was a widow and Stanley was an eligible bachelor! Though Stanley was quite a guy in the 'ladies department' he did not seem to have much luck with Mrs. Laing! We exhorted him to be nice to her, with quips like, 'You can receive the Governor's cup and sack the agents, Whittall, when you ultimately own the estate.' Stanley did not think all this was funny as there was a 30 year age difference between him and the proprietress!

There was a crowd of around 20 at the Malgolle party. Sanka had brought some of his guests. There were some very pretty girls. Two of them, Fiona and Ramani, I remember even through the passage of time. The others were planters from neighbouring estates with their wives, families and friends.

Sanka was a lavish entertainer. In those days the standard drink was a Gordon's gin and tonic in the morning, and an arrack and soda in the evenings.

Carlsberg and Tiger were the beers of choice. The younger

Oh this golden amber
water that's not so sweet
as a woman's lips but
a damned sight more
sincere

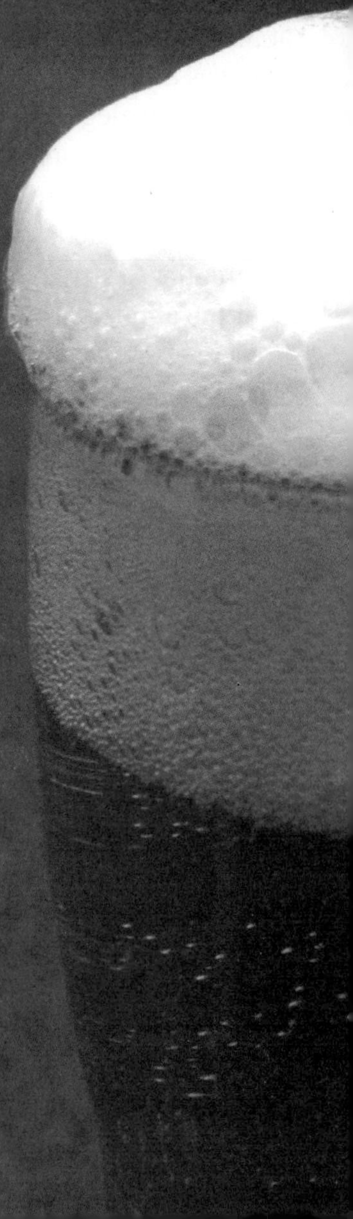

planters, due to restrictions in the financial department, opted for the beers manufactured at the brewery in Nuwara Eliya. Those present at Malgolle, however, preferred the more robust drinks.

Sanka took everyone by surprise, bringing out bottles of premium Dom Perignon Champagne in silver ice buckets as the starting drink of the day. Eyebrows were raised. We juniors asked Stanley who must have been an accomplice, if they had raided Mrs. Laing's cellar. Stanley retorted, "If we serve you guys a decent drink, it is Mrs. Laing's. If you are not used to drinking champagne, why don't you stick to the bloody arrack." There was no arrack at Malgolle. After prime champagne it was the choicest of whiskies and cognacs, served with sardines on toast and small fish cutlets.

Some were swimming. Meanwhile, Stanley was trying to teach the girls how to play golf on the mini golf course, and I assisted him from time to time in these lessons. None of us had held a golf club before! The ladies were in very fashionable swim suits showing off their ample endowments. The younger ones wore skimpy bikinis. When the young girls jumped into the pool, there were several volunteers trying to teach them the various strokes (swimming, I mean!)

A visitor had brought along an expensive transistor radio with taped music. The young girls and the planters started dancing. The day proceeded with much fun and frolics till an inebriated visitor accidentally kicked the radio into the pool. There was a hush of disappointment at this not because of the radio in the pool but due to the dancing coming to an abrupt halt.

Aelian, the all-purpose planter, undertook to get the radio repaired. I was wondering how he was going to do this. Everybody had confidence in Aelian's ability to sort the radio out. The party ended on a less lively note. It is usual at these parties for all those present to be invited for another get-together at a planter's bungalow in the neighbourhood.

Sometimes it was a string of parties, one after the other.

The next day I recounted this episode to the estate mechanic, Marshall. He told me, "Sir, bring me the radio and I will try to repair it, but don't hold out too much hope to the Big Master." I did not tell Aelian about Marshall's offer but handed over the radio to him all the same. Marshall walked into the tea factory and told the tea maker to inform him when he was lighting up the drier. I was wondering what was in Marshall's mind.

Marshall shoved the radio into the drier which was warming up, and opened the fan damper fully. He kept examining the radio every 15 minutes or so. After some time he brought it out and told me to switch it on. It crackled into life.

Marshall had simply used his common sense and made use of the temperature in the drier to take the moisture off. The heat, together with the gentle blast of air, had done the trick. Aelian had obtained an estimate from Siedles to repair the radio and replace the parts. I informed him that the radio was now as good as new. "What on earth did you do?" was his surprised response. Never one to take credit for what someone else had done, I told him about Marshall's ingenuity. Marshall was the most brilliant man when he was sober!

By this time, Aelian and Nalini were not only very fond of me but also realised that success would eventually come my way. What impressed them most was the total commitment that I had to my work. If I was told to supervise the night manufacture of tea, I left the bungalow at midnight and stayed over till 6am. Aelian paid surprise visits to the factory and found me fully involved in the work. Though I had worked the better part of the night, I made sure that I attended morning Muster. I have heard him extolling these virtues not only to the other assistants but to neighbouring planters too. The good tidings were conveyed back to me and I was naturally overjoyed. I did none of these things to impress him but merely because I enjoyed my work. To me it was almost an obsession to conclude any task allocated to the best of my ability. When working on an assignment, I lost track of time and drove myself and all those around me to the limits of endurance. Nobody complained because I was myself toiling along with the others.

I was, however, to damage this very high opinion that the couple had of me. This is the one incident in my whole planting career that I regret to this day. I have tried to make amends even though Aelian is no more, but have never been able to sufficiently atone for what I did.

There were three Assistant Superintendents on Galamuduna. Nihal Wickramasuriya was the senior Assistant, the other two being Ashley Fonseka and Clarence Fernando. Aelian had kindly permitted us the use of the tennis courts even when he was not present. One weekend when Aelian was away, all of us gathered at the big bungalow for a game of tennis. The usual procedure was for us to play a game or two, have a soft drink and go our separate ways.

On this particular occasion, Stanley Perera, our very good friend and neighbour and the Assistant Superintendent of Malgolle Estate, Dolosbage, joined us. We had a foursome: Ashley, Stanley, Clarence and I.

We played several games of vigorous tennis. Somebody asked me where Aelian was. I replied that he had gone away for the long weekend. Someone suggested that we should bring a few bottles and have a drink at the big bungalow and this was enthusiastically taken up by all those present.

There was no one in the big bungalow. I was the custodian. Hot water baths were had by all, using my bathroom and the visitors' bathroom. Evening clothes were donned and we sat down to have a couple of drinks. One drink led to another. The levels of the bottles were declining rapidly. Somebody suggested bringing a guitar and having a sing song. This led to a raucous evening. Our bottles were all consumed and the guys were asking for more! We dipped into a few of the bottles at the big bungalow. By around 2am everybody was too drunk to

go back home and all of them slept in the big bungalow.

All of us realised the next morning that we had trespassed completely on the hospitality of the De Silvas. The responsibility was mine. I did not know what to do. I had to tell Aelian what happened and ask his forgiveness. I was waiting for an opportune moment to do this, but I delayed doing so. This was the final betrayal of the trust and confidence placed upon me. This is where I learnt the lesson that unpleasant tasks must be attended to quickly. The delay resulted in eventually not doing it at all.

Aelian had come to know of the raucous evening. He was more disappointed than angry. To this day I feel the embarrassment and the betrayal. He summoned me to the sitting room. It was only the two of us. He took me to task. I listened to him in silence. It was too late for apologies. The time had passed.

He was extremely sad and disappointed in me. I told him, "What I have done is inexcusable. I know you cannot forgive me for this incident. I am sorry for what happened and I know that I have broken the confidence that you had placed in me. I am asking your permission to leave Galamuduna now. I do not want a certificate from you as I cannot hope to receive one after what I have done." I retired to my room to pack my belongings and leave Galamuduna as fast as I could. I took complete responsibility for what happened. Not once was any reference made by either me or Aelian to any of the other miscreants.

I was preparing to leave Galamuduna without a certificate for which I had strived for so long. I was taking a big risk walking out like this. Was I also a reckless gambler who was prepared to disappear to an uncertain tomorrow, without any concern? Was I gambling with my life? After all, I was the grandson of the President of the Suicide Club! I thought to myself.

I was saved from this dilemma. One hour later the butler came to my room and said that the big master wanted to see

me. I was too embarrassed to see him again. I wanted to get this over and done with. I wanted to vanish into the sunset and to an uncertain future.

This is where Aelian rose to the height of human forgiveness. This is where he was definitely on the side of the angels. He made me feel worse by his tolerance. "Herman," he said, "you don't have to leave Galamuduna, and I accept your remorse and apology. These things can be forgiven. You carry on as before. Don't do this type of thing again." I can never forget this man or his wife Nalini. They forgave me for the ultimate sin of betraying their trust. I resolved to stay behind for a few days. I knew that I had to go soon, and find myself a job, if that was going to be possible. This incident was not referred to again.

After the lapse of a few weeks I left Galamuduna. I did not ask Aelian for a certificate. However, he summoned me to the office before I left and gave me one. *'I recommend him without any reservation to anyone wanting a hard working and reliable Assistant'* is how he completed his certificate.

Thus ended the most regrettable and unfortunate incident in my whole planting career.

Harvesting the
green gold

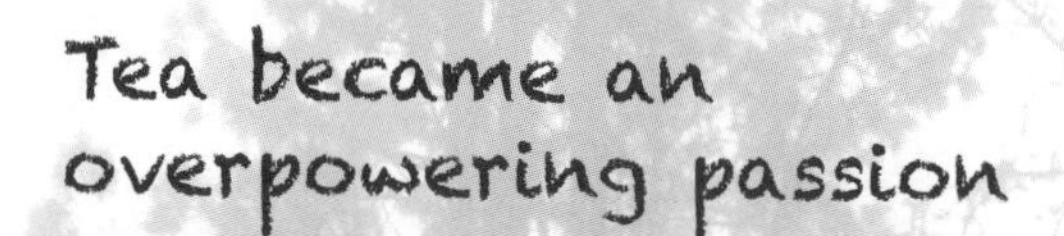

Passion is the secret to success

Sages, savants and saints have produced the best works on a feast of tea

ENTRY TO THE BRITISH PLANTATION RAJ

YATADERIA ESTATE, UNDUGODA

I felt that I had shot myself in the foot. Aelian would inevitably be asked about me by any prospective employer. I knew he would recommend me, but I could not expect him to be as enthusiastic as before the pre-tennis party period.

I had to get a job. I had no one to sponsor me, having decided never to seek the assistance of my highly placed and influential relatives.

The first step I took was to get a copy of the *Ferguson's Directory*, also called the Red Book. The big book contained the names and addresses of all the agency houses that ran the plantations. The names of the Directors and Managers of the estate departments were all listed clearly.

I had no recourse to a typewriter. There were no computers in those days. I made a handwritten draft of the application that I was to send to the agency houses. Many friends kept telling me that my efforts would be in vain without a proper introduction and a recommendation to the Agency House Chiefs. I had no educational qualifications that I could talk of. Not even the Senior School Certificate (SSC) - equivalent of today's General Certificate of Education - Ordinary Level.

So I used euphemisms like 'I possess a sound general education' leaving little doubt in the mind of the interviewers that, in the learning department, I was not the first in the queue. I got several type-written copies of Aelian's certificate marked 'True copy' and sent it along with my application which was a very brief one-page document, neatly handwritten with a thick-nibbed fountain pen. My handwriting was good. It differed from the normal. The writing was bold and straight, and nicely underlined where necessary.

Several applications were sent to leading agency houses. I received the usual quota of replies stating that 'We do not have any vacancies at the moment but your application will be considered when vacancies occur.' Some did not bother to reply.

I was sitting at my mother's ancestral home,'Nalagiri' in

Matara, anxiously awaiting the post every day. The postman had to ride the bicycle for about 100 yards up the drive to the house. I did not allow the poor man to strain himself! At 10am sharp, I was at the gate to collect the mail. This was my grandfather's house. Though he was no more, the headquarters of the Suicide Club remained in all it's regal grandeur.

I did not have to wait long. Within a few weeks I was called for an interview for the position of Assistant Superintendent by a leading British Company with large holdings in Ceylon. Harrison and Crosfield was the company. I was asked to present myself at their offices in Prince Street, Colombo, with all my certificates.

I shared the good news with some planting friends who kept telling me that I would have to get someone to speak to the Directors of Harrisons. This I was not prepared to do. I had gone this far without any external intervention and was determined to face the interview on my own. I knew my worth and I was confident I could handle the job.

The interview was scheduled for a morning. I was not overly nervous or apprehensive. I knew that if I was questioned on matters concerning plantations I could give competent answers. I walked into the offices of this staid British company and was ushered in by an aide. I gazed at the pictures adorning the walls and saw the list of Sterling companies managed by Harrisons. It was quite impressive. Photographs of the founders of Harrisons were prominently displayed.

I was asked to wait for the interview in the elegant room in front of the Manager's office.

Around six other candidates were also called for the interview. We started talking to each other. I found that most of the others were Assistant Superintendents already in employment, seeking to better their prospects by joining a reputed Sterling company. They were all very properly attired in dark suits with matching shirts and ties. I, too, was attired in a dark suit. They were all older than me and had better qualifications. I wondered what

MODERN TECHNOLOGY OWES ECOLOGY AN APOLOGY
THERE IS SUFFICIENCY IN THE WORLD
FOR MAN'S NEED
BUT NOT FOR MAN'S GREED
BECAUSE WE DO NOT THINK OF THE FUTURE
GENERATIONS THEY WILL NEVER FORGET US

chance I would have with these men who seemed to possess more experience than me. I resolved to do my best. I had the confidence derived from the long hours of hard work and the intensive training I received on Narangalla and Galamuduna.

My name was announced and I was ushered into the room. David Andrews was the Manager of the Estates Department. He was conducting the interview. Seated on his left and right were two others. He shook hands with me and introduced me to Rees Charles Hayworth Price, a tall, well-built Englishman with a prominent moustache, the Manager of Yataderia Estate, Undugoda. The other person was C. Mickey Abeysekera, whom I did not know then, but learnt later that we both went to the same school.

David Andrews explained to me that the vacancy was on Yataderia Estate and that the Manager would like to ask me some questions. Charles Price then asked me a series of questions on plucking, nursery management, labour management and my knowledge of the spoken Tamil language.

I could answer every one of the questions in very precise detail. I gave short comprehensive, staccato answers with absolute confidence. I had the right answers. Not once did they ask me of my educational qualifications or who was recommending me. The interview did not take more than 15 minutes. I was asked to wait in the outer room. I lit a cigarette and waited for the others to be interviewed and for the final verdict.

When the interviews were all completed, David Andrews walked out into the room and thanked all those who came for the interview. He looked directly at me asked me to stay behind.

I was ushered once again into David Andrews' room. "We are pleased to inform you that we have unanimously decided to offer you the job," said David Andrews, who proceeded to inform me of the salary and other terms and conditions. I could barely hear him. The terms, salary and other conditions were of no interest to me. I had got the job. That was all that mattered. Charles Price's asked me how soon I could report for work. I replied that I could be on Yataderia in five days. "Good," he said. We decided on a date. He asked me to report to his bungalow and invited me for lunch.

There is a lesson somewhere for aspirants to employment. To me, this was also a manifestation of the British way of doing things. No attempts at influencing. Not even looking at the single certificate from Aelian that I had brought along. These men simply judged me on the way I presented myself and the way I answered the questions.

I later learnt that all the other aspirants for the job had got many leading personalities to 'put in a word on their behalf.' According to Mickey Abeysekera, whom I met later, I was the only guy who came on his own merit.

I was to have this observation reaffirmed so many times in later years. I rose to some of the highest positions in the planting profession, culminating in my appointment as Regional Manager of the Nuwara Eliya region in charge of a 100,000 acres of Ceylon's best tea lands. Not once did someone 'put in a word for me.'

Rees Charles Hayworth Price's, whom I knew was largely responsible for selecting me, also sacked me after six months. More about that later.

My parents were overjoyed at the good news. We made arrangements to drive up to Yataderia. Henry Woodward Amarasuriya was the largest plantation owner in Ceylon. He was my mother's cousin. He heard about the news and came over to congratulate me. I showed him my letter of appointment. He said, "You know you are a very lucky fellow. How did you get this job? Did anyone speak on your behalf?" He was quite surprised when I told him that no one recommended me.

He then told my mother, "Isla, you must go up to Yataderia in my car. After all, that is the least that I can do for you." We

gladly accepted this offer, knowing full well that driving up for the appointment in Henry Woodward's car would be very impressive.

On the appointed day an Armstrong Siddeley, with a fully liveried chauffeur drove up to our house. I was trying to convince my mother that I should go up alone. She, however, insisted on coming along. My mother, now no more, was a tall, attractive woman who had lived some years in England and knew the Englishmen and their ways. She also felt that she should assist me to settle down in my new job.

The Armstrong Siddeley was Henry Amarasuriya's personal vehicle. There was an adjustable window between the driver's seat and the rear seat. When the window was shut the driver could not hear discussions taking place at the rear. My mother and I sat behind.

We drove up to Yataderia. I was thinking to myself, *Success has many fathers, but defeat is always an orphan.* It was Henry Woodward's Managing Director who told my mother that the only job I could get was the post of Conductor!

The car drove right up to the porch. Charles and Phyllis Price's came out to greet us. The stately car and the liveried chauffer did not go unnoticed by the Price's. My mother was very elegantly dressed in a saree. Charming the Price's was as easy as falling off a log for her. I was a not too reluctant a participant in this charade!

We went through the simple English lunch of roast beef, potatoes and some salad, topped up with a bread pudding of sorts. The roast beef was kept on a side table and Price carved the beef with a long carving knife. I declined the beer that was offered to me.

After lunch, Charles Price took us to the bungalow which I was to occupy. It was a wonderful, comfortable two-roomed unit with attached baths and beautifully maintained lawns. Price had cleaned up the bungalow for me. All I had to do was to move in. The view over to the Bible Rock was magnificent.

This was right in front of the bungalow. The only problem was that Charles Price could monitor all my movements from his bungalow which was not more than 100 yards away as the crow flies! This was very disconcerting, as I was to realise later.

A bungalow worker was available. He was Maria Michael, a Tamil Christian and an excellent man who became my friend through good times and bad. My mother set up the cooking utensils that had we purchased. She had also brought along some pre-cooked meals, sufficient for about two or three days. I insisted that she leave's the same day. I did not want to give the impression that I was being spoon fed. I was exhilarated on this first day and made a silent prayer to my mentors, Rama, Cubby and Aelian. My mother went back in the Armstrong Siddely the same day.

Price briefed me on the work for the next day. He wanted to meet me at the Nursery at 8.30am, after attending morning Muster.

There were almost 200 workers for Muster - around 150 pluckers and 50 sundry workers. Tissera was the Conductor in charge of dispersing the Muster by allocating different tasks to the workers.

Tissera was my immediate junior. Though Charles Price was the overall Manager, the usual *valame* (custom) on a plantation adhered to at most times, was that the Divisional Conductor was totally loyal to the Assistant Superintendent. He never went over the Assistant's head on any matter. He defended his immediate boss. The Assistant, too, never passed the blame on to the Conductor for any transgressions within the Division. The Conductor was responsible to the Assistant and the Assistant was totally answerable to the Manager. That is how the system worked.

Tissera started briefing me on Charles Price. "You have to be extremely careful of your dealings with the Manager," he said. "His biggest problem is that he listens to tales. He has

spies all over the estate. If you do not get on with the spies they will tell him all sorts of false stories about you and the Division. He has complete trust in these spies, he will listen to them and start harassing us." He then proceeded to tell me the names of the informants. "If you are too strict on the labour they will send him anonymous petitions. He will act on every one of them," Tissera warned me. "I have worked for several European Managers but Mr. Price is the most hardworking of them all. He knows the estate like the back of his hand. You must never give him excuses. None will be accepted. He is very keen on the tea nursery and if anything goes wrong there he will be very harsh on you. He was an Assistant Superintendent on Yataderia for almost 15 years on Northbrook Division, and he knows the workers and the staff better than anyone else," Tissera intoned.

He gave a special warning, saying, "Do not get too friendly with Mrs. Price. She is a wonderful woman but a little too fond of the bottle. She will come to your bungalow on a Sunday and ask for a drink. She will leave only after she has taken care of at least a couple of bottles of beer and a few arracks. If the Boss hears that she has been drinking with you he will never ask you directly, but will start finding fault with you on some other pretext."

Phyllis Price was a six-footer. She was dressed in somewhat simple cotton clothes and was perspiring heavily when she arrived at my bungalow after a long walk from God knows where. There was an all-pervading smell of perspiration and beer on her. I was later told that she was not averse to visiting the local moonshine maker for a morning tipple.

This advice coming from Tissera, who I later discovered could give anyone a run for his money in the drinking department, was quite hilarious.

I did not take these warnings too seriously. I thought that if I performed my duties properly, nothing else would matter. I later realised how wrong this was. Tissera was spot on in his assessment of Price.

I, however, decided to have an open mind and get on with my work. I met Charles the next morning at the nursery. Percival Ballale, the Senior Assistant Superintendent was also present and was introduced to me. I was asked a few questions about the various tea plants. I was being tested. He asked me to identify the different clones. I did this without much difficulty. Percy was watching this with some interest. I was asked if I had had breakfast, and I replied that I had before I left for the morning Muster. Price was happy at this reply. He then proceeded to take me round the Division, my area of authority. Percy asked me if he could pay a courtesy call on me before I left with Charles Price. I asked him to do so and told him that I would be looking forward to his visit.

I rode on a motorcycle provided by the estate, with Price riding in front on his own bike with his little dog, Pickle, perched on the petrol tank. This was to be a daily ritual. The first day was quite pleasant and uneventful.

Percy Ballale and his wife arrived in the evening for drinks. The three of us hit it off quite well from the very inception. We had a couple of drinks of local arrack which was all we could afford, and it went down nicely. I persuaded them to stay behind for some dinner. Percy's advice was far more subtle. He, too, told me that Price was a very hard worker and that he started his day at 6am. He had his lunch break at midday and went to the estate office at 1.30pm sharp. "You will be watched. The time you leave the bungalow, the time you return for lunch and the time you leave after lunch will be carefully monitored," Percy told me. "Even tonight he will be watching and noting the time I leave your bungalow." There was a feeling of oppression at these warnings. I thought that perhaps there was some over-apprehension on the part of Percy and Tissera.

In order to enlighten the reader on the long working hours let me outline a typical day on Yataderia. Morning Muster was at 6.30am. I left the bungalow at 6am, and returned for lunch at

12 noon. I departed the bungalow for the field again at around 1.30pm. The plantation work was over at 5pm when I marked the daily workers' attendance after the day was over at evening Muster. This went on till around 6pm. I then retired to the bungalow for a cup of tea at about 6.30pm before watching the sunset over the Bible Rock. This was an enchanting sight, which still haunts me and brings back nostalgic memories.

Then I had to start on the worst chore. I had to total the daily workers' check roll. This was a task allocated to me by Price for the first three months. I hated this work as I was very bad at adding and subtracting. For a man who was good at the task it took about one-and-a-half hours. For me to complete this task properly, because of my deficiency in arithmetic, it took around three hours. Even then I could never get the totals to tally. By 10pm I had now put in around 15 hours of work.

Fasten your seat belt. That was not all. Yataderia was also a rubber estate. There was a disease called oidium which affected the rubber trees. The trees had to be sprayed with sulphur dust when the dew was still adhering to the leaves. Sulphur dusting started at 1am and went on till 5am. You had now put in 19 hours of work. There was no respite. After sulphur dusting the daily routine thereafter resumed.

Sulphur dusting was not carried out throughout the year. It usually commenced in February or March, after the wintering of the rubber trees, and went on till the new leaves were established. This took two months.

I asked Percy Ballale if it was possible to take a few extra hours off in the morning after sulphur dusting to recover from a 19-hour working day. "Don't make that mistake," he warned. "The Old Man will visit you at morning Muster just after sulphur dusting to see if you are present." Tissera and the Dusting Supervisor also gave me the same warning. After some time, however, we found a way round it.

We left the dusting field around 4am, just to get some much-needed sleep. This was after briefing the Dusting Supervisor

to tell the Old Man if he visited the dusting field that I had just left, to get some additional sulphur or petrol for the machine.

Let me relate a story of how Price tried to catch me out on sulphur dusting. Charles Price was a great club man. Every Wednesday was the Kegalle Planters' Club Day. Price insisted that Percy and I visit the club on Club Days. In fact, he invited me to go with him and Phyllis Price in his big stately Humber Hawk Super Salon. Both Charles and Phyllis were six footers. They were an imposing sight. I was seated behind, sometimes with their daughter when she came for the summer holidays. The daughter had careless hands which found mine in spite of the intervening distance of the Humber Hawk Super Salon!

Percy and Irangani Ballale came in their Austin Cambridge. Percy always warned me to be careful of my drinks. "He will keep plying you with drinks. If you take drink for drink with the Price's you will be soon under the table." The club was a sight to behold. All the European planters were present. They seldom missed a Club Day. The men were all very smartly dressed in shirt and tie, and the ladies in cool, stylish cotton dresses. There was some special elegance in the way they held themselves, always erect and unapologetic. The Sinhalese ladies were in saree and blouse with some appropriate jewellery, but somehow were not able to carry it off with the same élan. They were a little shy and diffident. They always sat among themselves. The European wives joined us at the bar and had a good time.

Charles Warren of Golinda and Dick Levett of Parambe are a couple of those I can remember. Dunstan Cooray of Karandupona, Hercules Kalpage of Hatbawe, and Tiny Amarasekera of Etana were some of the Senior Superintendents. There were many juniors who came in early to play tennis. I, however, was not the tennis playing type, but contented myself with a game of billiards. These were convivial evenings where the cares of the world were left behind and all the seniors mixed openly with the juniors. Drinks flowed freely.

The billiards room was a place of congregation for the younger planters and the young girls. This is where I had a very unfortunate run in with Charles Warren of Golinda, a rotund, pompous Englishman. I was playing a game of billiards and that particular day the room was packed with pretty young ladies and the younger planters.

I smoke a cigarette while playing billiards, and used to leave it in an ashtray when it was my turn to play. On this particular occasion the game was gaining momentum and I forgot to leave the cigarette in the ash tray, and instead it was between my lips. In walked Charles Warren on his way to the gents' washroom. He saw the spectacle of my breaking the rules, playing with a cigarette between my lips. "Put that away, Herman," he screamed at me in everyone's presence of. I was furious at this arrogant order though I knew I had broken the rule. I had two options: sheepishly put the cigarette away or react in some other way. There was pin drop silence. All were watching how I would react. "If I burn the cloth, Mr. Warren I will pay for it," I said, and I continued with my shot. The audience was awe struck. Nobody talked to the British gods in this way. Warren halted in his tracks, looked at me without a word and went towards the gents' washroom. I realised immediately that I had shot myself in the foot!

Was I gambling with my job, a legacy from the Suicide Club?

A little while later he returned to the bar and reported this to Charles Price who popped in to the billiards room and saw me continuing with the game. He told a colleague to ask me to see him as soon as I finished.

I obeyed and realised that I was in for the high jump. "What happened between you and Warren?" he queried. I told him what happened and I apologised for the transgression, but explained that Warren had embarrassed me in the presence of everyone with his imperious order. "He should have called me to the side and told me to butt the cigarette without

screaming in the presence of everybody. I would have done this instantaneously," I replied.

"Serves the b----r right," said Price, to my utter relief, but he advised me, "Apologise to him before you leave the club." This I did, and Warren accepted the apology and offered me a drink. Not only the younger members but even some of the seniors who were not great fans of Charles Warren were elated over this incident and kept plying me with drinks. That night belonged to me!

The young, aspiring planting student must not get the wrong impression. I regretted this and such incidents are best avoided. I got away with it with the Europeans but had it happened today, the consequences would be far more serious.

Charles Price was always the first to offer me a drink. In those days we drank good coconut arrack. We, as juniors, returned the drinks and moved around talking to everybody.

If the daughters of the European and Sinhalese planters were present, there was always some mild flirting going on. The Sinhalese mothers watched over their precious offspring with hawk-like vigilance. The European girls were far more friendly and participated in the club's activities with enthusiasm. Many a tennis court romance began at the Kegalle club, only to end when the girls went back after the summer holidays!

Watching the tennis players was more exciting than playing the game. The English girls wore short flared white skirts well above the knees. When a particularly difficult placement of the ball was made by the other side, the girls ran to take the shot. The skirts flew up in the air, giving us a free peak of their white frilly panties! The young assistants partnering the girls were given strict orders to place the ball as far away from the girls as possible, just in order to make them run.

On this particular day, Price was sending me drink after drink and I was dispatching the drinks as rapidly as they came. Percy Ballale approached me at around 10pm and asked me, "Are you not sulphur dusting tomorrow?"

I replied that I was.

"Have you arranged for the sulphur and the petrol and the workers?" he asked.

"Yes, I will do it when I get back tomorrow," was my reply.

"You damned fool! Don't you realise that after midnight today, it is tomorrow!"

I looked at Percy, realising at once that I was in major trouble. "But I came with the Old Man. How does he expect me to sulphur dust when I have to go back with him?" I asked.

"That is not his problem. That is yours," said Percy. "I am warning you, leave the club now and start dusting. From the way the Old Man is acting he is checking to see if you will forget the dusting tomorrow, which is really after midnight today." It was only then that I realised that I had walked into a trap.

"Excuse yourself from the Old Man. I will take you back to the estate. Get the sulphur, the petrol and the workers, and start dusting. He is going to pay a visit to the dusting field. Don't tell the Old Man why you are leaving, just tell him you are off and come with me," he intoned.

I did just that. In the meantime, I realised that I had not drawn the sulphur from the Stores, nor arranged for the petrol or the workers. We drove back to Yataderia at breakneck speed. I rushed to the spraying supervisor, Sathiah's quarters, yanked him out of bed and told him to make a beeline with the workers to the dusting field. Only half the quantity of the sulphur was available. I mentioned this to Percy. "That does not matter, you use whatever is available. The Old Man won't know that you are spraying only half the required quantity. All he will observe is the smell of sulphur and you may still be able to get away with it today," was Percy's reply. I was now in panic mode. I pleaded, cajoled and pushed Sathiah who had a pronounced limp, to rush to the dusting field. We got there by about midnight and started dusting. By now I was completely sober. I told Sathiah to be on the lookout for the

A manicured staircase of tea

Big Master. At around 1am, Sathiah whispered to me, "Sir, don't look at once, but the *Periya Dorai* is watching us from a rock. Let's pretend that we have not seen him and continue with the work." He then shouted aloud to the labour to hold the nozzle straight so that the sulphur reached the rubber leaves. Price watched us for about half an hour, made sure that I was present and left. The angels were on my side that night!

The next morning we met at the Nursery. The Old Man was there before me. He had asked Percy if he had brought me back to the estate. Percy had replied with a dead pan expression, "Yes, Herman wanted me to bring him back because he had to dust today."

Price was happy at this reply. I rather suspected, however, that he felt a little disappointment at my having escaped the trap! I arrived at the nursery. "Sorry I am a little late, Sir, the dusting took some extra time," I said, piling up on my success of having eluded the trap!

I later discovered that this was a test that he was putting me through before he wrote the three-monthly 'Private and Confidential' report on my work. The report is normally sent to the Agents and onwards to the Principals in London. An admirable feature of the Old Man's confidential reports is that they were always copied to you. Good or bad. In this instance he stated: 'A very responsible and hardworking assistant.'

This is not to say that everything was sunshine and roses. During the three-month period he checked my work very carefully and on many occasions he pulled me up for shortcomings, at times unfairly. The workers on Yataderia were a lazy lot, and when there was heavy rain, they did not report for work.

"How many pluckers have reported for work today?" he asked me on an unusually rainy day.

"The turnout is poor due to bad weather," I replied at once.

"What the hell are you there for? Go to the lines and pull them out," was his reply.

He taught me that no excuse whatsoever was acceptable. Many years later, when the many assistants who worked for me fed me a similar excuse, I gave them the same reply: 'Go and get them.' A lesson was learnt.

The Old Man's great failing, as I was advised as soon as I joined the estate, was that he listened to tales and took anonymous petitions very seriously. When the labour and staff realised this weakness, they inundated him with a spate of unsigned letters. This was normally done by the villagers who, during the course of work, were reprimanded for bad work or for refusal of favours. 'Field No. 9 is full of weeds. The Assistant Superintendent never visits that area. The tea is covered with weeds,' and so on. Price went haring up the mountains looking for Field No. 9 to discover that the field was indeed full of weeds and the tea was smothered. We did not understand how he zeroed into areas where there were

weeds with such pin point accuracy. When Price was away in Colombo, Percy would act for him and he opened the mail. He saw these anonymous letters and warned me, and he took note of the Old Man's source of information.

We decided on a strategy to overcome this nuisance. We cleaned out some distant fields thoroughly and got some loyal villagers to petition the Old Man stating that the area was in a mess. Percy and I then watched with undisguised glee as the Old Man shinned up the hill to catch us out, only to come back frustrated and angry! These petitions were repeated once a month or so. Price began to ignore unsigned letters. The supporters, however, went overboard and went on to tell the Old Man how hard working and wonderful we were and how lucky he was to have assistants like us. The Old Man got suspicious. "You seem to be very popular with the villagers," he quipped sardonically.

The reader must not get the impression that we neglected the tea fields. The weather conditions on Yataderia were ideal for the growth of weeds due to the heavy rainfall. With the shortage of labour we could not complete the weeding round every month. Some areas were always prone to weeds. We attended to the backlog at the first available opportunity. Had he been a little less suspicious, we would have told him where the weeds were and also how we proposed tackling the issue. This was the problem with Charles Price. He belonged to the old school and did not understand that 'trust begets trust.'

He was also ruthless and unfair. I can remember the day I was supervising the plucking in Field No. 5 on Yataderia Division. I went to the field at 7.30am and walked from bush to bush examining and correcting the pluckers. My plucking fields were the best on the estate. And Price knew that. However, he arrived sharp at 12 noon, walked to the furthermost boundary and saw just one instance of bad plucking. "This is just not good enough. You are supervising the roadside tea and not the distant places," he shouted. I restrained myself, hoping that he would observe that this was only an isolated occurrence. The more I kept silent the more he continued shouting at me in the presence of the workers.

"Well, Sir, that is the best I can do. You do what you like," I said and started walking away from him. Charles Price was now coming through my ears, and I could take this no more. I walked away as I knew if I stayed there any longer I too would have responded in like mien.

Try to understand, reader, that I was supervising a field of 50 pluckers. There are 4500 bushes to the acre. I was walking from bush to bush, from plucker to plucker. I started at 7.30am. Price comes to the field at 12 noon. I was a dedicated worker. I worked very hard. I was hungry. He shouted at me in the presence of the labour. If he went on in this manner I knew I would have had to use the 'f' word on him. He cooled down immediately. "Herman, you are a good assistant but you must learn to take correction," he stated in a conciliatory tone.

"I am sorry, Sir, but I don't bluff you and I don't adopt one type of supervision for the roadside and another for the boundary. I worked my heart out in this field from 7.30am. You come at 12 noon and find bad plucking on one tea bush and scream at me in the presence of the labour. It is difficult to bear up such criticism," I replied, more subdued.

The same day he complained bitterly to Percy. "Herman does not take correction. He shouted at me today." Percy Ballale arrived at my bungalow to find out what had gone wrong. I explained what had taken place. "That's his way. Control yourself. Nobody has spoken to the Old Man like this. You are still on probation and you cannot afford to lose your temper, however nasty he is." I told Percy that we parted on not too bad a note and that as far as I was concerned I would be careful in the future. "He will never forget this incident," warned Percy. He and Iranganie seemed to be very worried for me. I think they realised that my days at Yatadería were numbered.

Again, was I too reckless? Price was surprised at my outburst. Nobody had retorted to him like that. Was I gambling once again with my job? The reckless streak bequeathed to me by the President of the Suicide Club kept surfacing at the most inappropriate times. On such occasions I had no thought for the consequences. I lived to regret my actions.

The workers and the staff were a witness to this exchange between the Old Man and myself, and were looking at me with open-mouthed awe.

There was one area where I was very weak. The adding and the subtracting of the check roll. I made many mistakes. The check roll was full of scratch marks and over-writings. Before the Old Man was able to spot this, I decided to ask Sathiah the Rubber KP to enter, total and complete the check roll in pencil. I was to ink it later. This happy arrangement went on for some time. I did not tell anyone of this and also swore Sathiah to secrecy. Another member of the staff with doubtful loyalties and a great ambition to improve himself brought this to the notice of Price. This was the beginning of the end for me.

I was summoned to the office. "Who enters the check roll?" I was asked.

"I do," was the reply.

Then he started examining the check roll with a microscope and discovered very slight smudges where the pencil markings were erased and inked by me.

"Look," he intoned, "I know that you get the Rubber KP Sathiah to enter the check roll and that you ink it later. I can quite easily get a statement from Sathiah that he is doing this at your request. Tell me the truth." I knew this was the end of the road for me.

"I am sorry Sir, I am very poor in my check roll work, and very tired when I get home in the evenings. The completion of the check roll takes me about three hours and when I have to supervise sulphur dusting, I do not sleep at all. So it is correct that I get Sathiah to help me with it."

The check roll is usually maintained by the Conductor. New Assistant Superintendents are told to occasionally enter the check roll merely to familiarise themselves with the labour force, to evaluate the performance of the pluckers who bring in low poundage and to check the attendance of the work force. No Assistant is asked to enter the check roll on a daily basis. But this was no excuse. I was just not able to complete the check roll properly and was now going to pay the price for it.

Price was now writing the second confidential report after the six months on Yataderia. A good report would have ensured my confirmation.

'Not carrying out instructions. Does not take too well to correction. Not suitable to be confirmed. Dismissal is recommended,' is what he stated instead. As usual, the report was copied to me. I knew that I had now received my marching orders. Price could not sack me. I had to be terminated by the agents, Messrs. Harrison and Crosfield. I was waiting for the letter to pack my bags and go home again, to a bleak future.

I showed the copy of the confidential report to Percy, the only friend I had. Percy and Iranganie went to a corner and had a hurried chat. They were really very concerned for me.

Percy joined me and told me the strangest story of my life. "Herman," he said, "both Iranganie and I have gone through this with Price. We have been saved by a holy man in Kurunegala, in the North Western part of the country, 25 kilometres from Yataderia. He gets into a trance and assumes the powers of the deity called Kambili. We would like to take you to him tonight. We are sure he can help you."

I was a non-believer, and I told Percy of my reluctance to seek divine intervention. He, however, prevailed upon me to accompany them both to Kurunegala. I was by this time clutching at straws and agreed. "What can the holy man do? The die is cast. I just have to await the letter of dismissal from David Andrews," I told Percy.

"We have got over more difficult situations in the past with the help of this holy man. You have faith and come with us," he replied.

We set off that night to Kurunegala. The solemn journey and the sincerity of two wonderful friends was calming and soothed my shattered nerves. Both of them kept telling me all the way to Kurunegala, "Don't lose heart. All is not lost. There are greater forces that you and I know nothing about. Price becomes insignificant against such awesome power," building up my hopes to a crescendo. By the time we reached Kurunegala, about two hours away from Yataderia, I began to have hope. The complete faith and belief that they had in the holy man began to have its effect on me. The closer we got to Kurunegala, more hope was kindled in me. The reverence they had and the wonderful friendship that they extended to me was just what I needed when all seemed lost.

They had sent a message to the holy man and he was ready when we arrived. The *devale* (temple) was in a remote corner on the outskirts of the town. We had to walk across a railway line, then cross a paddy field to reach it.

A kindly, middle-aged man was the *kapumahattaya* (holy man). He greeted Percy and Iranganie warmly. They introduced me to him as their best friend who needed help. He then told them to get someone who was able to chant *pirith* (holy melodious Buddhist stanzas). Percy had a person ready for the task. The holy man got into the regalia of the ritual.

The *pirith* chanting began to the gentle beating of a small drum. This went on for a few minutes and we could see the holy man gradually getting into a trance. His whole body started trembling and he began talking in a strange tongue. An acolyte who was able to interpret the language was also present.

"This child is innocent, he is hard working, but he is being recommended for dismissal by his boss," intoned the holy man. "The Boss has a grudge against him. He does not like

him because he argues with him," he went on. "Don't worry. The Kambili deity has agreed to help him. He will not lose his job. Before the sun rises to the peak (12 noon) you will find that a stranger will arrive to save him," was the strange revelation.

That was enough for the Ballales. "Don't you worry, everything will be OK," they said triumphantly.

"But Percy, how on earth can you be so sure? Who is the stranger who can arrive and how can he save me?" I queried, with a lack of faith.

"Herman," he admonished me, "the holy man has never failed in a prediction. You need to have faith. If you go on like this then nothing good will happen."

Percy was so certain that he took me to the Kurunegala club for a celebration. The confidence that the Ballales personified was infectious. I began to believe this prediction. After a few drinks I was on top of the world. We had one too many and I had to share the driving on the way back to Yataderia. We returned in the early hours of the morning. I was warned to walk back to the bungalow and give no indication to Price that we had both scooted off without permission. We were not allowed to leave the district without the Old Man's consent!

Back to being on my own, the old fears returned. How would I take my meagre possessions and leave the estate? Where would I go? What would I do with my little dog, Bullet? I had very little money with me. My parents did not know that I was up for marching orders. I could not even go to a friend's place with a little dog! With these sombre and melancholy thoughts, I resolved to wait till 12 noon.

Percy and I met at the Nursery the next morning. Percy was as cheerful as ever. I was biting my fingernails. Percy Ballale then got a message from Price at around 10am, asking him to attend to the mail and that Price would not be available. "Where the hell is he going?" I asked Percy. He did not know.

The *tappal* (post) man just then walked past the office. He

knew everything that was going on at the big bungalow. I asked him where the Old Man was going. "He is not going anywhere. He is expecting a master from Colombo for lunch," was the reply. I relayed this information to Percy. Just then a Ford Zephyr Six car whizzed past the office. Both of us recognised David Andrews, the Manager of Harrison and Crosfield. Percy told me this was a strange event. David Andrews never visited without adequate notice. "It is not yet 12 noon and this is your saviour," said Percy, remembering the words of the holy man.

Around 12.30pm I received a message through the *tappal* man asking me to come to the big bungalow as Price wanted to speak to me. Again, this was an unprecedented occurrence. "You know how to handle them," quipped Percy, having full faith in my ability to persuade.

Price was extremely charming, unusually so. "Have a beer, Herman," he offered, thrusting a tankard towards me. Why not, I thought, contemplating going down with a drink in my hand! A few pleasantries were exchanged. "David Andrews from Harrisons is here and he wishes to talk to you," I was told, and Price moved away. I then realised that Andrews had arrived not to sack me but to save me. Price's unusual charm and body language indicated that he was not having his way. I had to tread carefully, however.

David Andrews was the archetypal English public school man. Price was from a coarser background. I could sense this at once.

"I had great hopes for you when we selected you," said Andrews, putting me completely at ease, which is the hallmark of a good English gentleman. "Charles Price now wants you dismissed. He is one of our most senior superintendents. We have to abide by his recommendation as the man on the spot," Andrews went on very kindly. I knew at once that he was not going to sack me, because if he was, he would not be talking to me. I also realised that I should make it easy for him to bail me

out without in any way offending Price.

"I have worked very hard, Sir. In fact, I have worked my heart out for Mr. Price. But I have also made some mistakes. I have no excuses to give. Some of the lapses were because I was exhausted after work and did not have time to do the check roll. I am also not very good at the job," I said, addressing the main issue and also giving an explanation without seeming to do so.

"May I be permitted to apologise to Mr. Price, Sir, in your presence, and affirm that I will never make the same mistakes again? Could you please intercede on my behalf with Mr. Price and persuade him to give me another chance?"

One Englishman never lets another down but he also has a strong sense of justice. Andrews could not be perceived by Price as having a soft corner for me, and thus my appeal to Price through Andrews. Andrews was clever enough to understand how I was playing out this drama.

"Let's talk to Charles and see if he can give you another chance."

Charles Price was called back to join us.

"Charles, Herman says that he has made many mistakes and

wishes to apologise to you. He also says that he will never repeat these mistakes again and has requested me to obtain another chance from you to continue at Yataderia."

"Well, David, if that's the way he feels about it, I certainly don't mind giving him a further period of three months. In fact I rather like Herman," he lied. David Andrews now became very serious and addressed me strongly.

"OK, Herman, Mr. Price here is willing to give you another chance. This is the final opportunity we can give you. I hope to have improved reports on your work in the future."

Andrews was in the wrong job. Running estates was too small for him. He should have been an Ambassador for the Court of St. James! He stood by Price and he did justice by me, as he realised that this was a mere clash of personalities.

"Thank you, Sir," I said to Price, and thanked David Andrews for giving me a hearing. I was playing out the charade to the end! David had already decided what to do. I went out of my way to help him do it. Rees Charles Howarth Price was not a happy man.

I did not want to seem triumphant and walked out of the big bungalow with my head bowed.

The stranger had arrived before the sun rose to its peak. I was saved as the holy man had predicted. I went back to Percy, a little cockily, and told him that Price could not have his way and that I was given a further three months' reprieve. "Serves the b----r right," said Percy irreverently, knowing full well that Charles Price would not be happy at this outcome.

Who is this holy man, and who is this deity that saved me? These were the inexplicable questions that were passing through my mind. At that moment, however, nothing mattered, only that I got another lease of life. Born a Buddhist, understanding completely the simple logic of the Buddha's teachings, I had the opportunity to delve into some aspects of the unknown. Some may call it the occult. All I can say is that if it was so, then it was a benign power that intervened on my behalf. In later life I was also to see the awesome power of Jesus Christ. But that is another story. I have tried to delve into these strange occurrences in my own life from my own experiences and have come to the conclusion that there is a confluence in all the great religions. But this is the story of the Plantation Raj. Perhaps one day I will tell you the stories of the occult and how the only force that was able to combat the dark and evil forces was the power of Jesus Christ. But that was much later, and must be another story.

Percy and I met at his bungalow after David Andrews left and we reviewed the day's proceedings. Percy was wise in the ways of the world. "The Old Man will never get over what happened. He is somehow going to get rid of you, so be careful." He told me that Andrews had made a mistake by giving me a further trial period of three months.

I resolved, however, to do my best and work my heart out on Yataderia. I kept out of sight, but worked round the clock. My crops had increased. The estate was clean. The labour was well under control. Price had nothing to say.

One day he came to the pruning field and saw me pruning the bush bare bodied, my shirt tied around my waist.

“What the hell are you doing?” he asked me, surprised at my pruning.

“This man Karuppiah, when I pulled him up for bad pruning, told me this was the best he could do, and if I didn’t like his pruning, I should show him how I wanted him to do it. I am simply responding to his challenge.”

Price looked at me with some respect, inspected the bushes that I had pruned, found the work to be extremely satisfactory, and summoned Karuppiah, too, to inspect the bushes. He admonished Karuppiah, “The Master has shown you how to do it, now do it without argument.”

The labour sometimes does this to you. When you turn on the heat, they innocently ask you to show them how to do it. I knew my pruning and could prune as well as any good pruner. When I took the knife from Karuppiah, the first thing I did was to re-sharpen it. Thereafter I proceeded to prune carefully but fast. Each pruning cut was clean and resembled a 25 cent coin. This is the ultimate in pruning.

There is a lesson here: ‘Never ask them to do something that you, yourself, cannot do.’

At the end of three months, however, he sent another report to David Andrews. ‘Has shown an improvement in his work, but still not up to my expectations and requirements.’

As usual this confidential report was copied to me.

Upon receipt of this report, David Andrews summoned me to Colombo. “Herman, I am sorry, but it is quite evident that Charles Price does not want you around. When two people cannot get on, the lesser of the two must go.” Andrews realised that Price was pursuing a vendetta against me. “I will see that you are employed in a similar capacity. The best thing for you to do is resign from Yataderia. I will see what I can do for you soon” he said.

I told him that I would resign immediately. I asked him for a piece of paper and wrote out my resignation there and then. I thanked him for all the courtesies extended to me and asked his permission to leave.

"What do you propose to do?" he asked me.

"I will look for another job," I replied. Bold and reckless decisions one might say. I was not inclined, even when faced with dismissal to beg. At the Suicide Club you walked away and risked losing everything.

"Wait a moment. I will see what I can do," he said, and reached for the telephone. He spoke to Herbert Whittal, a Director of George Steuart and Company. "Herbert, I have a young man with me. He was Charles Price's SD. You know Charles Price. He could not get on with him. But I think the lad has potential. Can you see what you can do?"

Herbert Whittal apparently told him that right at that very moment he had a vacancy and an interview was going on to fill it. He told Andrews to send me to George Steuart and Company immediately. I walked across from Prince Street to Queens Street, where the interview was going on.

The candidates summoned for the interview were all seated in the lobby. I was summoned last. Herbert Whittal was dressed in a white shirt and white slacks. Charles Nicholson was in serge shorts and an expensive cream coloured shirt, and David Labrooy was dressed like Herbert Whittal. The three of them were going to decide my fate.

The vacancy was for the position of Assistant Superintendent of Dunsinane Estate, Punduloya.

Nicholson seemed a kind man, very civilised and polished. He questioned me closely on various aspects of plantation work. Having worked for Price, I was quite thorough with all plantation practices. I was able to answer all the questions confidently, and I knew I gave the right answers. I was asked to wait outside in the lobby. The other candidates, all well dressed and in very formal attire, were also waiting for the final result. I was the only person who went into the interview in slacks and shirt sleeves. After all, this interview was not something I had come prepared for. I was wondering if they would ask me why I left my previous job on Yataderia. I decided that I would

tell them the truth. That I was sacked. They never asked me this question. I am certain that David Andrews would have told Herbert Whittal the reasons for my departure. That is how the 'old boys' network functions. The deliberations went on for a long time. The others who came to the interview knew that my name was not on the list of those to be interviewed. I was also quite inappropriately dressed for the occasion.

All the others interviewed were asked to enter the room of Herbert Whittal. I was left out.

After about five minutes they all trooped out of the room, not looking too happy. I was recalled about 10 minutes later. They made sure that the other candidates left the premises before I was called.

"We have decided to offer you the job. Mr. Nicholson, the Manager, is proceeding on overseas leave and we need you to get there as soon as possible," said Herbert Whittal, the Director. I was offered a much higher salary. I agreed to report to Dunsinane Estate in five days. Perhaps after the satisfactory interview, they realised that I could move in to take the job without delay. The others were all employed and would have needed to give notice to their employer before leaving. On this occasion my being unemployed worked to my advantage! In their perception I may have demonstrated both my suitability and availability for the appointment.

This was another example to me of the British sense of justice and fair play I came to know of. David Andrews, God bless him, realised that I was a victim of an unjust man, and was not going to allow me to go home empty handed. He may have told Herbert Whittal that I was an unfortunate victim of a clash of personalities. The European community in Ceylon was very closely linked and Price's idiosyncrasies were well known.

Honest labour wears a lovely face, I thought to myself and made all preparations to report to Dunsinane Estate, Punduloya.

"The goddess Badrakali is said to be the patron of vengeance. Badrakali is, however, not appeased by mere devotion and veneration. If you want a favour from her she has to be satiated with a blood sacrifice."

HARRY UGLOW AND THE THREE LIMES FROM THE SAME STEM

A STORY OF THE OCCULT

This was an incident connected to my stewardship on Yataderia. So I would like to give it to the reader before moving on.

The story of the holy man from Kurunegala got around. Ceylon is a land of no secrets. It is also the land of the occult. A survey of the practitioners of the occult in the South have revealed that within an area of 10 square miles there were over 2000 practitioners of this mumbo jumbo. The Sinhalese referred to them as *devas* (gods). Devil or deity, these dark forces have immense power and can harm humanity. The practitioners of these black arts have the ability to marshal the evil forces for good as well as for evil purposes. They are called *kattadiyas* (witch doctors) or *yakaduras*.

Each one of these witch doctors harnesses the power of a particular demon or deity. They do this by chanting melodious and, sometimes rasping stanzas, singing the praises of the force from which they obtain special favours. Sacrifices are made. Statues are erected, dressed up in gold and silver, and the forces are worshipped devoutly. The demon or deity then does the bidding of the witch doctor. Usually a vow is made and the devotee, after achieving what he came to the witch doctor for, fulfils the vow with great veneration. The witch doctor also charges a fee for the work performed. If you are gullible and loaded with money, he ensures that you come to him again and again. And then you are truly hooked.

I do not wish in any way to give the reader a discourse on the black arts. This is, after all, a story of the British Plantation Raj! However, I have had some very special experiences with a man who could neutralise the effects of the supernatural. That must, some day, be another story. It will be a story far stranger than fiction.

My tale is how a planter (I will call him Senaka, although this is not his real name) went to a witch doctor to sort out a problem that he had with his Director in the head office of a leading agency house in Colombo. I have concealed the

identity of the protagonists in this funny drama with the occult. These things are done in the stealth of the night, like visiting twilight ladies. Nobody likes to talk about these nocturnal visits to marshal the dark forces.

Harry Uglow was a planter who later rose to become a Director of a large agency house in Colombo. Uglow was a tall, buff Englishman with a handlebar moustache, and who was bountifully endowed with a strong physique. He was a kindly soul, whose stern demeanour belied a great sense of humour. My friend could never work that one out. He was a pitiful bag of nerves at the mere mention of Harry Uglow's name. Like a quivering jellyfish!

Uglow was giving the 'treatment' to Senaka, who tried everything in the book, and some things outside it, to please him. These Colombo directors held the power of life and death over the planters. My exasperated colleague swept the roads when Uglow came and mowed the lawns to perfection. He bought the most expensive flowers to place in Harry's bedroom when he came to visit, Harry was wined and dined with the choicest of food, yet he did not relent. He twisted his handlebar moustache, rolled up his sleeves, and gave my friend the works.

Senaka was not the brightest of planters. He may have been doing everything right but the results were not forthcoming. His estate was running at a loss. This is what concerned Harry Uglow the most. If you delivered the goods, you could get away with some indiscretions. If you did not, they gave you hell. I have seen plantation managers reduced to a miserable state when dealing with these directors. When I met my friend at the club I advised him to take stock of the situation and find out from Harry Uglow exactly what he wanted from him. Senaka recoiled at this suggestion.

"Are you mad? How can I ask him that?" he queried incredulously. I realised then and there that the mere mention of Uglow's name was sending shivers down Senaka's spine.

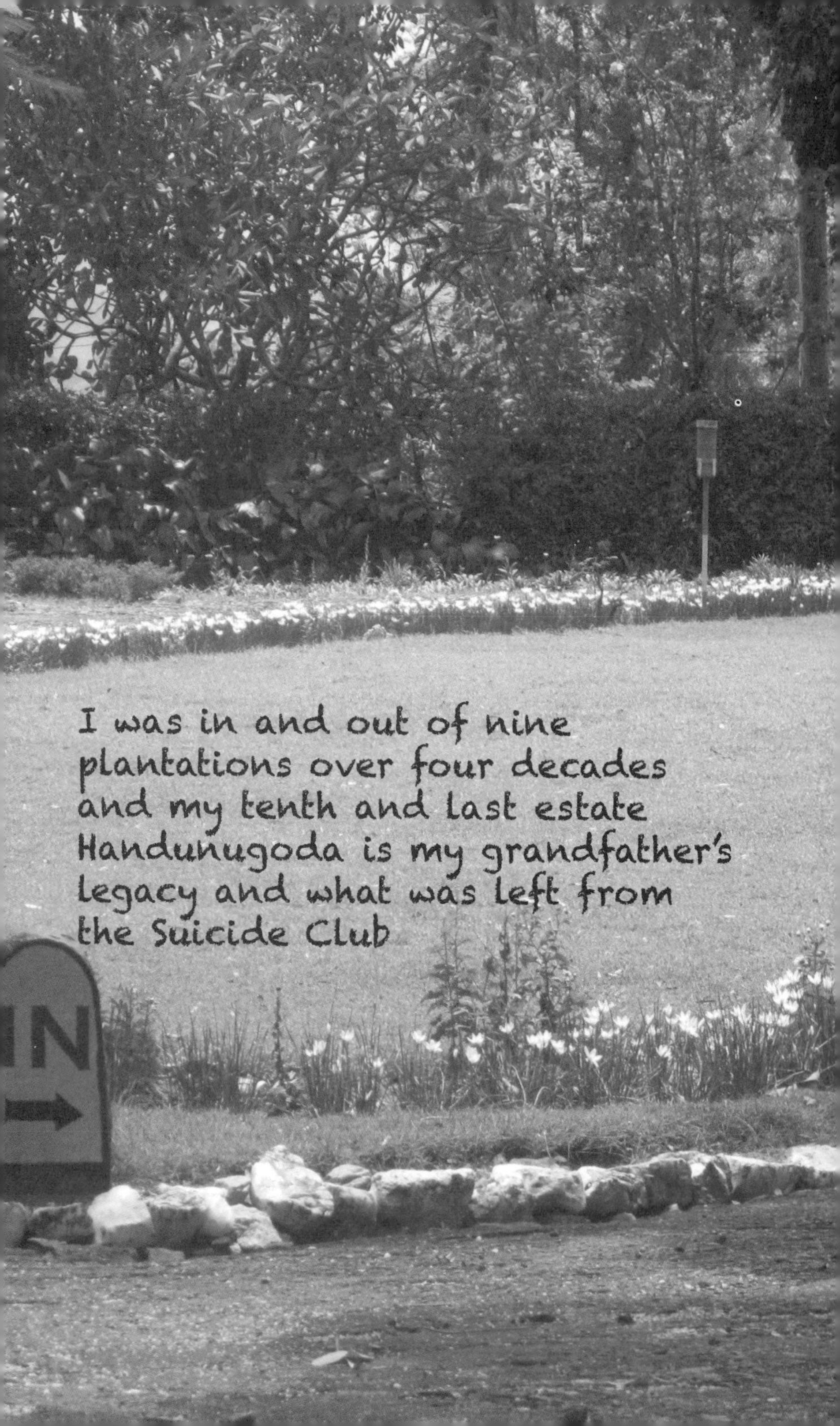

I was in and out of nine
plantations over four decades
and my tenth and last estate
Handunugoda is my grandfather's
legacy and what was left from
the Suicide Club

Senaka was not willing to take a chance. He had no gambling spirit. He was hedging his bets. He had not heard of the Suicide Club!

He resolved to go down the mumbo jumbo route. Witch doctors are visited by devotees for a number of different reasons. If you are sick you go to the witch doctor and he ties a charmed string on your wrist or hangs one round your neck. If you want to harm an enemy, the mumbo jumbo man has a recipe for that as well. Problems of unrequited love are grist to his mill. He will ask you to bring a lock of hair from the unfortunate girl upon which he then casts his spell. If that is difficult to obtain, he will ask you to bring some soil from the abode of the girl, which is then worked on, and you are supposed to throw it back to her in her compound and make sure she walks over it. She then comes under the spell of this master of evil. If you want to win the favour of your boss, you are given some chanted oil which you are supposed to apply to your forehead when you go to meet him. He then comes under your spell.

There are more serious and dangerous rituals that can even cause the death of your enemy. The goddess Badrakali is said to be the patron of vengeance. Badrakali is, however, not appeased by mere devotion and veneration. If you want a favour from her she has to be satiated with a blood sacrifice. The Sinhalese Buddhists will not think twice about putting to death an innocent cockerel or a goat to feed the blood lust of Badrakali. She personifies evil. Almost every Buddhist temple has an area (*devale*) devoted to these purveyors of evil. Worship the Buddha for peace and deliverance. Go to Badrakali to knock your enemy out!

How these black arts came to be compatible with the teachings of the Buddha I know not. It is, however, a fact that the Sinhalese Buddhists will not think twice about visiting *yakadura* and receiving the benefit of his bag of tricks. Indeed I feel that these demons are venerated more than the Buddha,

the Enlightened One.

These gods are also said to be a part of Hinduism. I have known Tamil plantation workers frequently seeking the solace of witch doctors. The odd Christian, too, slips in to these abodes of evil, under cover of darkness!

It is the *Bible* that clearly establishes the existence of evil. The Devil is the force of evil, God the immaculate force of peace and tranquillity. The Buddha, who gained emancipation and enlightenment, also deals with evil forces (*mara*).

The Buddha is not in the favour-granting business. Jesus Christ, too, cannot be bribed with a sacrifice to do anybody's bidding. If you wish to obtain the blessings of these two major religious teachers, all you have to do is to follow their Commandments. The Commandments for the Christian and the Buddhist are not at all dissimilar.

Oops! Sorry. I am straying into a field that 'angels will fear to tread.' This is not a religious lesson or discourse on comparative religions. It is the story of a desperate man going to a witch doctor to obtain some relief from his irate boss!

By this time my story of the holy man from Kurunegala had done the rounds (I will always think of him as a holy man). I did not go to him to cause harm to Charles Price, but to seek solace for myself.

Senaka had heard the story of this external intervention. He considered me to be an expert in this department. I was like a consultant to the art and craft of the mumbo jumbo! He came to me one day and told me that while he was visiting his village and discussing his problem with a village elder, he was asked to lay his problem before the village witch doctor. "This man will sort your problem quite easily," the village elder had told him. Senaka asked my views. Knowing how desperate he was, I advised him to go right ahead, though I would have advised him against this if he asked me the question today. I told him that he should allow the witch doctor to try his hand at turning Harry Uglow round!

Senaka, his wife and the village elder made an appointment with the witch doctor. Somehow these appointments are given at an ungodly hour of the night. The village elder had paid a visit to the mumbo jumbo man to obtain the appointment and to explain Senaka's dilemma. The elder was told to ask Senaka to bring three large limes growing on the same stem for the ritual. This was a difficult proposition as three large limes growing on the same stem are a rare phenomenon.

Senaka was seen scouring the lime trees in the area to get this rare commodity. He finally found what he wanted.

Harry Uglow had summoned Senaka by that time to the Colombo office. This is usually an ominous sign. You are never summoned to Colombo for fellowship or goodwill. He read this as the final stage in his planting career.

Meeting the witch doctor assumed some urgency. Senaka visited him in the night with his wife and the village elder. The witch doctor had an acolyte standing by. The acolyte then

started reciting some stanzas, rising gradually to a crescendo. The mumbo jumbo man, now in the full regalia of the ritual, gradually got into a trance. Senaka was watching with goggle-eyed apprehension.

"Give me the limes," he ordered. Senaka gingerly gave him the precious, innocent limes that were going to save his job! The man, now in a full trance, held the limes to his lips and whispered an incantation which was barely audible. This went on for about 30 minutes.

Senaka was finally given clear instructions. "When you go to meet the *suddha* (white man), have the limes in the right side pocket of your pants. Try your best always to maintain hand contact with the limes when you are talking to him." This was not an easy feat and needed practice. An Englishman dislikes someone talking to him with his hands in his pockets.

Senaka and his wife had some practice runs in his house under simulated Colombo office-like conditions. The practice

The Kovil is a place of sanctity for the Tamil plantation worker

sessions went on till he became quite adept at squeezing the limes and talking at the same time. Senaka became quite an accomplished lime squeezer! He was now ready to take on Harry Uglow. The sorcerer told him, "Do not worry, do as I have advised you and you will have the *suddha* eating out of the palm of your hand!"

I can still remember poor Senaka. He wore tight-fitting long pants which were somewhat badly tailored. Hip-huggers would describe them aptly. I wondered how he was going to perform this act in his tight trousers, without the limes bulging out of his pocket!

Senaka was now armed to the teeth. Tight-fitting, hip-hugging pants and three large limes were all a part of his armoury. The inoffensive planter was ready to battle with the unsuspecting Harry Uglow.

On the appointed day, Senaka went down to Colombo for his meeting with Uglow. His wife accompanied him. Senaka parked his car outside the head office and started walking to the Director's office. "Remember the limes," his wife reminded him. Senaka gave her the thumbs up signal and walked jauntily to meet the Director. He was confident that the chanted limes would save his bacon.

A peon (an office aide) ushered him into Uglows's elegant room. These Englishmen are the epitome of courtesy, even when they are pronouncing the death sentence. "How are you, Senaka?" started Uglow. Senaka warmed to this cordiality and gave an extra squeeze to the limes in his pocket.

"The results on your property have been very unsatisfactory over the last two years," Harry Uglow went on. Senaka realised that the riot act was just about to be read out and that the cordial discussion was soon coming to an end. He went at the limes in his pocket with gusto.

This is when the unthinkable and the unanticipated happened. A lime disentangled itself from the stem and plonked to the floor with an audible thunk. Senaka panicked.

He was in a bath of perspiration. He was speechless. He could not pick the lime up. It started rolling on the floor and Uglow saw the spectacle of the rolling lime. "Oh, Senaka, what are you doing with a lime in your pocket?" At this, Senaka had mumbled something about going to the market and buying some limes. Harry Uglow was quite amused at this planter with limes in his pocket. He was not to know that Senaka had two others concealed in the same place.

Harry Uglow was later to remark to a colleague, 'Oh, these local planters are funny guys, they walk about with limes in their pockets!' He was not to know that the limes were a part of the armoury that the local planter used to neutralise the impending disaster.

Strangely, Senaka was given another lease of life. Perhaps Uglow saw Senaka's pitiful state after the discovery of the fallen lime and had mercy upon him. "I am giving you a further period of six months. If I do not see an improvement you will have to find yourself another job." Senaka went back to his wife who was waiting anxiously in the car.

When he told his wife about the mishap with the fallen lime, she declared her brutally, "You can't even squeeze a bloody lime without dropping it on the ground."

Senaka was sacked in six months.

TeA
CEYLON TEA
TeA
CEYLON TEA

ON THE ROOFTOP OF THE ISLAND

DUNSINANE ESTATE

Penniless, with hardly any money but with a lot of experience and a letter of appointment from one of Ceylon's best companies, I went up to Dunsinane in a Volkswagen car that was hired and paid for by a cousin of mine. My meagre belongings all packed into one suitcase, and with my beloved Cocker Spaniel, Bullet, I commenced my journey to a new future.

On the way to Dunsinane I had to stop over at Yataderia to collect the few items of cutlery and crockery that I had acquired while being there, and kept at Percy Ballale's bungalow on Northbrook Division. I was hoping that I would not meet Price on my way to Percy's. Of course he had to be the first person I bumped into on the climb to the Northbrook Bungalow. He greeted me cheerfully. "Where are you off to, Herman?'"

"I am reporting to my new job at Dunsinane Estate," I replied jauntily.

Price seemed visibly unhappy. He may not have realised it then, but his dismissal set me on a path to a life-changing future. He had later told Percy that I should have been without a job for a longer period. 'Herman will never learn a lesson this way.'

I arrived on Dunsinane on schedule at around 12 noon. The Nicholsons were waiting for me. I was greeted by Charles Wilson Bennet Nicholson with great warmth and kindness. He introduced me to his charming wife, Margaret. We exchanged a few pleasantries over a soft drink, which I accepted. Nicholson had a gin and tonic, the typical Englishman's morning drink.

Charles Nicholson came from a more refined mould. He spoke softly. He had a soothing voice. He was dressed in black serge shorts, highly polished brown shoes, and a very expensive-looking shirt. He never addressed any of his assistants by their Christian names. I was Gunaratne to him.

He described the plantation, and the company that I came to work for, in great detail. "Dunsinane is the largest continuous block of tea in the island. It belongs to the Estates and Agency Company in Great Britain. We have no other plantations in Ceylon, but we

have a number of estates in India, including Seaforth and High Forest. The Chairman of the company is Sir John Arbuthnot, a member of the British Parliament from the Conservative Party. Lord Tweedsmuir is another Director. He sits in the House of Lords."

I was now being given a full insight to the British plantation ownership structure, and to the realm of British peers and noblemen. "Sir John visits the plantation every year over Christmas. He would like very much to meet you when he comes. You have a bright future here."

Nicholson elevated Dunsinane in the eyes of a newcomer like me, to a very high altitude. I realised that I had entered the true British Plantation Raj. He was also impressing upon me that Dunsinane was the *crème de la crème* of the plantations in Ceylon. All this was done without any pomposity and in a very matter of fact way. It also became quite evident to me that very high standards in all aspects of plantation life were maintained on Dunsinane and were expected of me as well. We sat down to lunch over which he told me that I would be staying with them that day and could move into my bungalow the next day. Margaret Nicholson was a most caring host and made me feel quite at home. By this time I had mastered the use of the usual array of 'weaponry' on an Englishman's dining table! I did notice, however, that this was being carefully observed by the couple. If Nicholson was surprised at my lack of baggage to take up the new appointment, he did not show it. Saving money for a rainy day was not in my catalogue of 'things to do.' I was not interested in the acquisition of baubles. I spent lavishly at the club and eventually acquired a good wardrobe.

After lunch he retired to his bedroom for the traditional 40 winks. I was shown into my bedroom. "We will drive up to your bungalow in the afternoon at about 3pm. I will also take you to the tea factory," he added.

I was ready sharp on time. We got into his spanking new Austin Cambridge car driven by young Jebamalay, an excellent driver. This was quite different from the way Charles Price welcomed me on the first day. The atmosphere was thoroughly relaxed and the climate was invigorating. He showed me that I was a very vital member of his management team.

"You will be in charge of 300 acres on Factory Division. The previous Assistant was Brian Faithful, an Englishman and an all Ceylon rugby player. He left us to join one of our plantations in India."

He continued, "I have two other assistants. Earnest Dalgety is the Senior Assistant. He will be acting for me when I go on overseas leave shortly. He is the Assistant on Middle Division. The other Assistant is Ian Austin, a Scotsman, who is in charge of the Upper Division. You will be the third Assistant. We had four assistants in the past, one on North Division. He was Terrence Donnan. This post has now been suppressed." He briefed me thus about the senior staff on the estate.

"You will be totally responsible for all the work on Factory Division. A motorcycle is provided for supervision, but you must not use it in the mornings. Supervision is best by foot. The motorcycle can be used in the afternoons to come down to the factory and to visit your colleagues. We have a wonderful club, the Punduloya Planters' Club, which you must join. I will ask Austin to take you there and make you a member." Never 'Ian,' it was always Austin or Dalgety or Faithful. "I will introduce you to Dalgety, who will be the Acting Manager for six months," he went on.

I was delighted with the Factory Division bungalow. It had two rooms, a cosy fireplace and resembled an English cottage. It was cut off from the rest of the estate and was in the uppermost part of the plantation. This was a welcome change from Yataderia, where Price could monitor my movements just by listening to the drone of my motorcycle! The cook was standing by to welcome me, and my dog was given over to him for one day. I did not wish to burden the Nicholsons with my pet.

We then went to the tea factory. Dalgety, the acting man, was present. I was introduced to him. He was a tall, slim Englishman. I could sense that Dalgety and I would get on well together. The Dunsinane factory was one of the largest in the island. We walked around it and inspected the standard of green leaf coming in. Nicholson was very keen on tea manufacture and insisted on a very good standard of leaf. "Good tea is made not in the factory but in the field," he emphasised. I understood this maxim thoroughly.

Thereafter he took me round his sprawling empire, which extended from Nuwara Eliya to Punduloya. It was truly awe-inspiring. The scenery was spectacular. Verdant green tea fields with gushing waterfalls, manicured lawns and typical British buildings and estate bungalows.

Dunsinane was like a picture book. I knew instinctively that this was where I have always wanted to be. During this brief tour he asked me many questions, not so much to test my knowledge but to find out if I would have any problems in handling the task allotted to me. With my confident answers Nicholson appeared completely reassured.

We reached the big bungalow at around 6pm. He asked me to have a bath and join him and his wife for drinks at 7pm. Sharp at 7pm I walked into the sitting room. The Nicholsons, dressed very formally, greeted me warmly and invited me to join them for drinks. I, too, was very smartly dressed in grey flannels and a blazer and an expensive tie.

The drinks trolley was laden with a choice array of drinks. I opted for the safety of a beer. We had a very pleasant chat about my family and my previous experience on the estates where I had learnt about the business. He gave me a brief outline of Dunsinane and mentioned that he would be proceeding on overseas leave, and that when he came back he would be working very closely with me. In his own way he was making it very clear to me that Earnest Dalgety was only the Acting Superintendent and that he would resume full charge upon his return.

Dinner passed off without any untoward event. The only snag was the dessert. A huge pineapple was served intact. I did not know how to handle this. Since the dessert was first served to Mrs. Nicholson I was relieved. She simply removed the top slab of the pineapple and scooped up the fruit salad that was inside and served it onto her dessert plate. I was wondering if I had to cut up the pineapple and eat a piece! I was saved from this *faux pas*.

After dinner we had a premium Cognac and I retired to my room. Thus my first day at Dunsinane passed. I was happy and knew that I had gone through the first day's proceedings well.

I settled into my bungalow on Factory Division the next day. The financial department was rather depleted! I had to feed myself, the cook and the dog and was wondering how this was going to be achieved without hard cash.

I started gently probing the cook. "Is there a grocery store close by? I do not want to go to Nuwara Eliya to buy provisions as it will take too much time." Nuwara Eliya was unthinkable, without cash!

To my great relief, Karuppiah the cook told me that there was a well-stocked co-operative store on the estate.

"The only items the co-op store does not have are beef and frozen foods, but they have all types of tinned fish." he informed me.

"That's OK, Karuppiah, I have been eating beef every day in Colombo. I am sick and tired of eating beef and chicken, so fish would be a welcome change."

Having sorted out the culinary department, I happily set to work.

I am going to deal at some length with my first days on Dunsinane just in order to provide the aspiring planter an insight into what it was like during the days of the British Plantation Raj.

Vengadasalam was the all-powerful Head Kangany of Factory Division. I was repeatedly and carefully advised by

Nicholson that it was important to get on with him as he had total control of the labour force. Vengadasalam was a very kind old man but it became quite evident to me after some time that he clearly called the shots on the estate. He was the proud owner of an Austin A30 vehicle which was immaculately maintained. The labour had enormous respect and regard for him. I later learnt that this control was largely due to the fact that the majority of the workforce belonged to his caste.

I may have reigned as the Assistant Superintendent of Factory Division, but Vengadasalam clearly ruled the Division. I was going to tackle him very carefully but I needed to take full control of the estate.

Vengadasalam accompanied me on my field rounds the first few days. We had long chats in Tamil. I told him very clearly of the improvements I wanted effected. I solicited his support to achieve this end. He gave me his fullest cooperation. I started tightening the screws very gradually. He never went round the fields but knew exactly what was happening on the division. I rather suspected that he was given a daily report of my activities.

Though the Head Kangany never went round the fields, he jealously guarded the check roll. He was always present at morning and evening Muster. The workers were deployed for different works at morning Muster and their names recorded in the check roll at the evening Muster. I attended both these daily events and I realised that this did not appear to meet with Vengadasalam's approval. "Master does not have to come for Muster every day. The previous Masters never came for Muster," he gently told me. I disliked being told what to do, even from the powerful Vengadasalam.

"That is OK, Head Kangany," I replied, "I must get to know the work force and how you are deploying them for the different jobs. I need to study the pluckers and the poundages they bring in so that we can improve the performance of the pluckers bringing low poundages."

My first task was to improve the productivity of the estate and I could only do this by increasing the output per plucker. Vengadasalam was not too happy at my eagerness, but on that I was not willing to compromise. "Don't bother about me, you carry on as before, but let me carefully study what is going on," I told him. I spent a lot of time in the plucking field. Sixty per cent of the expenditure on the estate is on plucking, and it was therefore my belief that at least 60 per cent of the Assistant Superintendent's time should be spent on the plucking field. Today, sadly, no one pays attention to plucking. This has led to the dramatic decline in the organised plantation sector.

My attention to the plucking fields brought immediate results. The crops started increasing rapidly and all the fields of Factory Division started looking good. This became evident to Ted Dalgety and he complimented me on the improvements on the estate.

Ian Austin was the other Assistant on the Upper Division. I met him while going round the fields. He was a young, extremely good-looking Scotsman, married

Their meagre belongings are hung on trees while plucking tea

to a Ceylonese girl. Gillian was his wife, the daughter of the Trinity College Principal. Gillian was a very pretty woman. Ian invited me to his bungalow for drinks. He had heard from Dalgety that I was doing a good job on Factory Division and was curious to know what type of a guy I was. I rather suspected that Dalgety had gone a little overboard about my work and had told Ian that I was a thoroughly competent Assistant. He referred to Nicholson rather affectionately but irreverently as 'Nico.' After making sure that I was the correct type of guy who would fit into the British plantation club culture, Ian told me, "You must join the Punduloya Planters' Club. Club Day is on Wednesday and we have afternoon tea there." There was no compulsion whatsoever to join the club but it was made clear that joining it was an essential part of a planter's life. This proved to be so true. You met senior planters to whom you could go for advice. You met Trade Union leaders and politicians. It was at the club that you kept abreast of what was going on in the country, in the otherwise cloistered plantation world.

When I learnt from Nicholson that all the other senior executives were Europeans I reconciled myself to being treated a little differently as a native. I remembered S. W. R. D. Bandaranaike's audacious paradox in Oxford. He was high born, but there was an inner portal at Oxford that he could not walk through. It was then, he says, that he arrived at the solution to the problem: 'Before I become their equal I have to be their superior.' This was the way he gained instantaneous acceptance by making the most eloquent and spellbinding speech at the Oxford Union, of which he later came to be accepted as the Secretary. I had no visions of being anyone's superior. I would be happy if I was accepted for what I was.

To my complete surprise I was treated by Nicholson and the others in a very friendly manner and the association was extremely cordial. Nicholson never had the others for dinner at his home. He would regularly invite me. So did Ted Dalgety and Ian Austin. Always by myself I rather felt that they were

vying with each other to be warm and friendly. In fact Nicholson told me that very few Ceylonese had been invited to the big bungalow. S. Thondaman, the Minister and leader of the most powerful trade union in the plantation sector was an exception. Ian Austin was a teetotaller. Dalgety and I used to knock down some pretty big gin and tonics. Drinking sessions with Dalgety sometimes extended to the early hours of the morning with his wife staying up and joining the conversation. With Nicholson, I was careful. Two whiskies and dinner was as far as I would go.

Both Dalgety and Nicholson would bring all visitors to my Factory Division first, because it was the showpiece of the estate. They accepted me simply because I was competent and I had the ability to converse with them fluently. There were instances when Nicholson had corrected the spelling of a European Assistant!

I say all this just in order to impress upon the aspiring planter the need to be competent in the allotted task. It is then that there is acceptance. Though I was invited to the bungalows of my colleagues I would not invite them to mine. I was leading a very spartan existence and did not possess the array of cutlery and crockery with which they tormented me during meals. In the course of time they started dropping in uninvited and spending long hours with me, talking away in to the night. They accepted me for what I was. I was extremely grateful for this. In regard to partaking of my meagre fare of string hoppers, *roti* and *thosai*, they went about it with great gusto, and I rather suspected that they were enjoying themselves with the spicy food Ceylon is well-known for.

I spent almost six years on Dunsinane, being promoted from the most junior role to a Senior Assistant. This is not intended to be an autobiography, so I will not bore you with any more details. These are tales from the Raj and not a personal story!

No tale of the Plantation Raj would ever be complete without describing in detail the visit of the Chairman from overseas. Our Chairman was Sir John Arbuthnot MP, and a leading figure in the Conservative Party in England. His colleague on the Board was another peer of the realm, Lord Tweedmuir.

Sir John made it a point to visit Dunsinane every Christmas. The whole plantation was put on full alert. Buildings were painted, lawns were closely mown, roads were swept, vehicles were polished and the plantation presented a picture of impeccable tidiness. Sir John spent almost 10 days on the estate. Nicholson used to mutter under his breath that his Christmas season could not be enjoyed with Sir John staying with him. It was customary for Sir John to first visit the agents in Colombo, George Steuart and Company, to receive a full briefing on what went on. He also made it a point to meet S. Thondaman, the most powerful man at the time, who was my friend and the leading trade union leader in the plantation sector. He also paid a courtesy call on the political leaders at the time. These meetings were carefully arranged by the agents. When he arrived on Dunsinane, he was fully aware of the political and economic policies of the government in office.

Sir John was a tall, gaunt man who was quite aware of his power and position, and for 10 days he made Nicholson a nervous wreck. He would want to see the engineers, the Visiting Agent and other senior and neighbouring planters. They were all invited to dinner and the Nicholsons had to host dinner after dinner every night for the duration of his stay. I could see the Old Man was a bundle of nerves and felt very sorry for him indeed. He used to slip away when Sir John was either resting or asleep just for a little consolation and light-hearted banter with us.

Sir John was quite adept in the alcohol department, and had an enormous capacity for liquor. He would start with gin and tonic in the morning followed by liqueurs after lunch. The lunches would finish at around 2pm, throwing the whole household into disarray. The dinners were another affair altogether.

There were two days set aside for dinners for the Assistant

Superintendents and their wives. One upon his arrival, and the other just before he left.

Let me try to recall one such dinner party. The Nicholsons would send us a printed note stating that Sir John Arbuthnot MP, and Chairman of the Estates and Agency Company, would like to have the pleasure of inviting Mr. and Mrs. Austin for dinner. This sent the plantation wives into a tailspin. They started preparing for the dinner party one or two days before the event. New sarees were bought, hairstyles perked up, face lotions applied, and rehearsals carried out with matching lipsticks. Sarees, shoes, jackets and shawls to match were bought from Butani's in Nuwara Eliya.

When the day arrived the ladies looked so elegant and beautiful that Sir John would gaze at them in sheer admiration. The ladies were fully aware of their attraction and turned on the charm for the British peer. The husbands would have to live on bread and water for the next few months!

Sir John would set the tone for the evening. A particular brand of Scottish malt whisky from the Isle of Skye was his preferred choice. He would put on a special display for the ladies. Nicholson would gently warn us to go easy on the drinks. He himself was very abstemious and had only a few whiskies. Despite Nicholson's warning, we got in some extra shots of Chivas Regal just to get into the right mood. The tables were laden with Lobster Thermidor, specially ordered from the East Coast, and other choice meats. Prawn cocktail was the starter. Margaret Nicholson would also produce the most delightful desserts. The discussions would centre on the politics of Ceylon and the plantations in general.

On this particular day at the dinner table, he suddenly asked us assistants whether we would like to read the *Daily Telegraph*. I was later to learn that this was a Conservative newspaper. When the question was asked of me I replied quite frankly that I had hardly any time to read the *Daily News*. There was a deathly hush, during which Nicholson looked at me as if I had brought mud into the sitting room! Not willing to read the *Daily Telegraph*, the Conservative newspaper was an act of sacrilege! He then went on to tell us that when he met the leader of the United National Party (UNP) he had asked him for a campaign contribution. "Do you think we should support him?" he asked.

Having made one *faux pas* I replied that it would be advantageous to the plantation interests to have the UNP in power. He persisted, "Do you think that I should make a contribution?" I replied that I would consider it imprudent for a foreign company to engage in supporting one party or the other in Ceylon.

"I agree with you. If a foreign company supported the Labour party in the UK we would be very cross with them." Was he testing us? I was past caring with quite a few whiskies under my belt. I rather think that that Sir John admired this frank expression of views. This proved to be correct, because he later sent me for a fully-paid training in tea manufacture to Aislaby Estate, Bandarawela. He told me that he was satisfied with the reports on my work from Nicholson and that he looked forward to better results in the factory on his next visit. I was to give him results that even surpassed expectations.

To the aspiring planter my advice is to speak your mind. It is not what you say so much as the way in which you say it that matters.

The time had come for the British planters to leave the island. A wave of nationalism was sweeping the country. Nationalisation was in the air. The British plantation companies were uncertain of the future. There were rumblings of discontent in the country. Earnesto 'Che' Guevera was leading a revolution in Bolivia. The main cry of the revolution was land reform and re-distribution. An insurgency in the South of Ceylon adopted 'Che' as their symbol of liberation. 'Che' was the romantic hero who sacrificed a Cabinet portfolio in Cuba and went across to Bolivia to lead a peasants' revolt.

The insurgents called themselves the 'Che Guevarists.'

The insurrection was to come a few years later.

Coming events were casting their long and ominous shadows. Nationalisation followed some years later. This was going to be the biggest disaster for the plantation industry in the island.

Ted Dalgety loved Ceylon but decided to go back to the UK. Nicholson retired after 35 years on Dunsinane. Ian was promoted to Dickoya Estate, Dickoya. He chose to remain in Ceylon as his wife Gillian was Ceylonese and he wished to stay back and watch the unfolding drama. Ian and Gillian, too, eventually left the island but that was some years later.

Some very remarkable and not so remarkable managers succeeded Nicholson over the next couple of years, until I was appointed the Manager of Dunsinane many years later. I was the youngest Manager to attain this exalted position.

Farewell to the Nicholsons from the staff of Dunsinane. I am seated to Nicholson's right, next to his daughter, Diana

H/C
'I not married will look after lady like my own. When master go visiting I will do nice things to lady, like Partridge lady I will do nice, nice things also to nice nice places. I am also good massaging. I rubbing lady nicely in nice nice places, very slowly. More rubbing more lady liking.'
A. Suppan's application for a job

THE PLANTERS' CLUB

THE CLUB WAS THEIR TEMPLE, BACCHUS WAS THEIR GOD

Clubs dotted every sub-district of the plantation areas. It was almost compulsory for a planter to be a member of a club. You were gently advised not only to join a club but to ensure that your club bill was paid on time! My mind went back in time to the Suicide Club. Not only were the members the wealthiest people in the country but they settled their debts which were considerably higher than club bills, on time!

The Punduloya Planters' Club was where we all met. Ian Austin invited me to the club and enrolled me as a member. The attire was quite formal in that era. Coat and tie for the men and the ladies in all their finery. It was the unwritten rule that all the Managers, along with their wives attended the club and also ensured that the assistants did so too. We did not need much persuasion to be present! Club Day was eagerly looked forward to.

This was even more so when the plantation daughters came with rosy cheeks for the summer holidays. Tennis was the easiest way to the hearts of these fresh English roses. Many a romance began during the summer holidays, only to end when they went back to school.

The Punduloya Planters' Club was a powerhouse. The most powerful people in the country at that time made it a point to be present on Club Day. Mr. Unamboowe was the Provincial Chieftain (*Rate Mahattaya* or RM) during the British period. He was responsible to the British government for the administration of the Province. He was a regular. A fine bridge player, he could also account for a few large and strong whiskies. Completely refined, well-mannered and very friendly to us juniors, he was my friend, guide and adviser on all matters. RM was a genial man who recounted many tales from the British Raj. He was also an unrepentant and uncompromising nationalist. We got on perfectly, as we thought alike on most matters. He showed his distaste for some British planters who attempted to treat the Ceylonese as inferiors. I was his kindred soul. I must confess, however, that I never had any problem with my British colleagues. This must have been because I never sought to be too familiar with them. I realised then that 'familiarity breeds contempt.'

Politics was the main subject at the club, with politicians from all shades being members. The political party of the planters was the United National Party (UNP). To be a member or a supporter of the left wing Sri Lanka Freedom Party (SLFP) was unthinkable. If you were a supporter of the SLFP you were the odd man out, a renegade. They looked down their noses at you. I belonged to this category, and I made no apology for my convictions. Word, however, got around that I was the only SLFP supporter among the planters. J. D. Weerasekera, elected from the SLFP as the Member of Parliament for Kotmale, became my very close friend. JD was an urbane politician, loved by all, and much sought after by the planters for prestige and favour, but never did he get a vote from them. He knew it. He was appointed the all-powerful District Minister for Nuwara Eliya, the most prestigious plantation district in the island.

Ceylon's most powerful man was Saumyamoorthy Thondaman. He was the 'King Maker.' No political party or government could be elected to power without the support of Thondaman. He had complete control over 500,000 votes. He was the Proprietor of Wavendon Estate in Ramboda and Meddegoda Estate in Udahentenna. A long-standing tennis playing member of the Punduloya Club, he demonstrated the will to win even on the tennis court. While all of us maintained a veneer of camaraderie on the courts, Thondaman made it very clear that he was playing to win.

He was in his late 60s when I first met him. He was fast on his feet, and did not give a quarter. He usually played at the net and was unapologetic and ruthless about where he placed his shot, whoever his opponent was. Even opposing ladies in mixed doubles were par for the course for him!

He was also a great and steadfast friend. The Tamil plantation workers held the balance of power in Kotmale. JD, who always won this seat, could never have done so without the support of

Thondaman who always backed the UNP. In Kotmale, however, he sent a subtle message to his plantation workers: 'Vote for Weerasekera. He is my friend.' To Thondaman, friendship transcended politics.

After tennis he ordered round after round of drinks and kept everybody regaled with stories of the inner workings of the power structure in Ceylon. Prime Ministers and Presidents were at his beck and call. He could get anything done from the power elite in the capital city. He became my friend and saved me from many a disaster in later life. He also appointed me a Chairman of one of his corporations, until I was unceremoniously removed, in his absence, by the then President Ranasinghe Premadasa for supporting the development of the handloom industry. This I did at the request of the former (and late) Prime Minister, Sirimavo Bandaranaike, who showered wholesome praise on me in Parliament. I was sacked for doing my job a little too well.

A digression here: I was seated in Parliament when it was the time for the Textile Ministry votes to be taken up. Sirimavo Bandaranaike was the first woman Prime Minister of Ceylon and the world. She paid high tribute to the work I did to revive the handloom industry in Attanagalla, her electorate. Pat Gunasinghe, the Secretary of the Ministry, was seated by my side. He nudged me on my shoulder and said, "You will be fired tomorrow." I was sacked by the President. But that is another story.

The other senior members of the Punduloya Planters' Club were the Mathavan brothers, Thondaman's nephews and owners of the sprawling Meddetenne Group in Punduloya; Brian Richards, the Manager of Sheen Group, and his wife; the Nicholsons of Dunsinane; the Dalgetys of Dunsinane; Gordon Macsporran, a Scotsman on North Punduloya; and a few Ceylonese assistants. There was also Vyapury Murugiah of Choicy Estate, a rather coarse planter who, despite having fun poked at him for his mannerisms, carried on regardless!

Members had to take turns to provide tea for all those present. Some senior members and their wives produced an elaborate

array of short eats, with some strange sounding names. Angels on horseback, canapés, spring rolls, curry puffs and delicious chocolate cakes. In time we learnt that, when some particular members were providing the fare, we could feast on the food and skip dinner. We all made it a point to be present. The younger members produced more modest fare. This was all taken in good spirit. However, a degree of competition developed between the seniors. If the Nicholsons brought chocolate cake, another would bring a chocolate cake together with an elaborately decorated ribbon cake with loads of icing. We, the juniors, were the beneficiaries of this friendly rivalry.

The club had an excellent billiards room. Intense billiards games were played with the seniors and juniors competing fiercely. The fun, however, was at the bar. As the evening shadows lengthened, the arguments rose to a crescendo. J. D. Weerasekera and I were on one side and the more conservative planters on the other. The ladies, too, joined in complaining about the way Ceylon was going, with increasing nationalism sweeping the land. There were one or two snooty English ladies who looked down their noses at not only the Ceylonese planters but also at their own countrymen. The story did the rounds at the club that the Richards' only spoke to the Nicholsons and that the Nicholsons only spoke to God! One of these so-called upper crust ladies was one day heard complaining how difficult it was to find a decent chef. We overheard her saying that she had placed an advertisement in the *Daily News* for a good cook and that she was eagerly awaiting a response from the applicants. We decided to have some fun at her expense.

The advertisement duly appeared:

Wanted: A cook for an up-country Senior Planter's bungalow. Must be conversant with Western dishes, pastry, cake and bread making knowledge necessary. Only those with good testimonials must apply with copies of all certificates. Very good salary for the right person.

She was asked by the other planters' wives to pass on the applications to them so that they, too, could recruit one from the many applicants who were bound to apply. These discussions went on at the club and we juniors overheard the animated conversations. The advertiser was asked to select the candidate of her choice and bring the other applications to the club so that the other ladies, too, could select from the list.

We decided to apply.

This was our application, which we knew was going to provide some mirth and titters from the others.

Anthony Suppan (Cook Appu)
Diyagama Bazaar
c/o Arunachalam Barber
Diyagama
Agrapatna

Honoured Master and Lady

I giving cousin brother address in Diyagama. I god fearing Christian 57 years but young looking, sure Lady/Master will like. I having 30 years experience with European masters and ladies. Trained by Partridge lady on Diyagama East. She very good. I do nice, nice things to her. She very love me. I look after Lady very nicely when Master going visiting.

Bread making, cake making simple for me. Partridge lady teaching me everything. Western courses, Eastern dishes also intercourses. I look after the full bungalow. Two second servants under me. Supervision of whole bungalow my duty. I only entering lady bedroom. I make bread pudding, yorkshire pudding caramel and blancmange pudding. When native masters come I make rotis and string hoppers. They like my cooking but I

not like these local foods. Dont you know these Sinhalese masters they not like Europeans, eating with hands not with spoon fork European style. I like work only for European masters and ladies. Sinhalese masters always asking for pol sambol and beef curry not rost beef and potatoes, what to do they not like Europeans.

I not married will look after lady like my own. When master go visiting I will do nice things to lady, like Partridge lady I will do nice, nice things also to nice nice places. I am also good massaging. I rubbing lady nicely in nice nice places, very slowly. More rubbing more lady liking. I making food alone for party. No taking leave. Only Sunday 2 hours to go Church. I pray for God look after master and lady.

If lady select me for the job I do all the things like in this letter.

I am obedient servant.

A.Suppan.

We drafted this application on single ruled paper and posted it from Agrapatna. The envelope was an old one, and it gave the authenticity of a typical cook (*appu's)* application for a job. This was a joint effort of two young assistants and to this day their identity is unknown.

The lady who placed the advertisement arrived at the club the following Wednesday. She was livid. She brought along the application to show the others. "Look at this application and the impertinence of this fellow," she complained. The ladies all got into a huddle to read the application. There were titters of restrained laughter. The recipient was not happy. She was also not the most popular plantation wife in the area. She was a little snooty and the others revelled in her discomfiture. 'Serves the bloody woman right,' was a sentiment that was echoed outside earshot.

The authors of the application realised what was going on and were overjoyed at the result. We walked around asking them what the huddled discussions were all about but there was a stony silence. The English don't betray their own. Not in their presence, anyway.

These were the lighter moments. The club, however, was an important institution where ideas, information and knowledge were exchanged. There never was any social distinction between the seniors and the juniors. They bought you drinks and you made sure that you returned the compliment. This became a fairly expensive affair as the seniors were drinking whisky and soda and we juniors were knocking down Old Arracks! They were thoroughly civilised, though, and gave you the last round of drinks before leaving the club.

The club also had a very elegantly designed and equipped Ladies' Room, with a double bed for the tired planters' wives to rest after a game of tennis. The beds were decorated with a special material brought out from England. Pastel blues and pinks with a frill of lace adorned the bed sheets and it was

all very delicate and spic and span. Eau de Cologne, expensive face creams and powders were stocked on the dressing tables. Dainty pictures and lace curtains were all a part of the Ladies' Room décor. This area was forbidden territory to the men.

Some of the younger members, however, used the Ladies' Room on non-club days for more indelicate and untidy purposes. The information was somehow leaked and there was unrestrained horror at the activities of the younger members. 'Who dares to desecrate the sanctity of the Ladies' Room?' It was not only the local planters who participated with these ladies of easy virtue. There were a few European assistants, too, who put the Ladies' Room to good use. The room was thereafter locked up and the key was in the possession of the ladies' convenor! I rather suspected that the seniors were somewhat envious of the roistering that took place on non-club days. "Where do these girls come from?" they asked, only to be met with a deafening silence. The incidents were strongly denied.

One particular day I was invited to dinner by an English planter and dropped in at the club for a last 'one for the road' before proceeding home. The sight that unfolded before me would have sent shivers down the spine of the ladies. Out popped an English colleague, bare bodied with the daintily frilled bed sheet wrapped round his waist and a cigar clenched between his teeth, followed by a pretty young lady who had more 'span' than 'spic.' She had daubed herself with the expensive perfumes and was looking quite at home in the Ladies' Room. I rather suspect that my friend had also given her a few shots of arrack. She had no inhibitions and was caressing my friend tenderly. He did not seem to have a care in the world, and seemed to be vicariously happy that the staid British Ladies' Room was being put to good use by him. I had a couple of drinks with them and left the club. On the way out, around 1am, I saw a man in a sarong and a black coat lurking in the corner. I asked my friend who he was. He winked at me

Natives were not
allowed to disturb
the sanctity of
these sacred halls
with their footfalls

and replied, "An uncle." A euphemism!

We enjoyed the irreverence of the way in which the Ladies' Room was used by the men. Had the uptight ladies seen my colleague, with the sheet wrapped around his waist and the cigar between his teeth, I am sure they would have had convulsions! All this was done with the knowledge of the club keeper, Hassan, who was handsomely rewarded for his silence!

Apart from these youthful indiscretions, the Punduloya Planters' Club was a place where some of the biggest industrial disputes were settled by Thondaman, drinking his whisky and soda and nonchalantly asking the plantation workers to return to work after a long and strenuous strike.

Each plantation club had an annual tennis tournament followed by a dinner dance. Members from all the plantation clubs in the hill country participated at these tournaments. A billiards tournament was also held concurrently. The club was a hive of activity. The ladies were dressed in their finery. The young British girls, dressed in shorts displaying their contours took to the tennis courts. They taunted us younger members with their attractive legs. Some tennis court flirtations were par for the course and were generally ignored. These affairs seldom lasted.

There were many planters' clubs in the

area representing each geographical sub-district: Dicksons Corner Club for Udapusellawa; Maturata for the Maturata sub-district, Talawakelle Tennis Club for Talawakelle; and Agras Club for Agrapatna. The Darawella and Radella clubs were the main rugby playing venues.

Two clubs, however, need special mention. The Nuwara Eliya Golf Club and the Hill Club. Membership to these clubs was restricted to Europeans only. The Golf Club, however, later condescended to take in local golfers. Only the upper-crust Ceylonese were allowed to play golf there. Nicholson, my boss, was the President of the Nuwara Eliya Golf Club for a number of years. I used to accompany him there on a few occasions but joining the club was by invitation. Golf was an expensive game and Nicholson never thought it fit to invite me, realising perhaps that the membership was too expensive for a young Assistant Superintendent. I later went on to become the President of the Nuwara Eliya Golf Club.

The Hill Club was a residential club, and it was positively out of bounds for the Ceylonese. Dark-skinned creations of the Maker were clearly told that 'Thou shall not enter.' I saw nothing wrong with that. If the Europeans wanted to be among their own and discuss the vagaries of the weather and other inconsequential things, that was their problem. However, what turned my stomach was the host of Ceylonese, mostly Sinhalese, clamouring to join the Hill Club. They would do everything within their power to seek entry. When the European population started dwindling, the hallowed portals were thrown open to a few select Ceylonese who were from the uppermost crust of society. They strutted round the Hill Club flaunting their esoteric status. 'We are at the Hill Club,' they would say to us lesser mortals, almost as if they were invited to stay at Buckingham Palace. I, too, was invited to join by the then President, Vernon Ratwatte. I declined, not because I had an aversion to joining the club but simply because I found it unnecessary to become a member of both the Hill Club and the Golf Club, which offered similar facilities. After returning

to Ruhuna, my birth place, I joined the Hill Club as residential facilities were excellent for golfing holidays with my sons and grandsons.

The Hill Club took you back in time to Victorian England. Her Majesty the Queen of England was the Patron of the club. Toasts were drunk to her health on ceremonial occasions. The Presidents and Prime Ministers of Independent Sri Lanka did not seem to exist. There was a hushed silence within the precincts of the club. You had to wear a coat and tie for dinner. I saw no problem with that because Nuwara Eliya was cold and a coat and tie were not out of place. A hot water bottle was discreetly placed underneath the blankets. There was a crackling fireplace in the room. All very comfortable and so British! The club staff floated around, their footfalls barely audible, serving their Masters' every whim and fancy. The serving staff wore white cotton gloves. You were transported to a new world. For a moment you thought you were in England. The Ceylonese have now taken control of the club and thankfully the same high standards are being maintained. I recently asked the General Manager about the reason for the success and high standards of the Hill Club. His reply was quite simple: 'It is due to the strict adherence to the old rules.' The Ceylonese, mainly the Sinhalese, seem unable to run a club without bringing down the standards built over many decades. The Hill Club is the exception.

Most of the other plantation clubs have closed down and some have been demolished. An essential part of plantation life vanished with the demise of these venerable institutions.

"The Club was their temple and Bacchus was their god," intoned Minister Hector Kobbekaduwa on the floor of the House of Parliament, when the Bill for the nationalisation of the plantations was moved and passed. "Even the most Buddhist of Buddhist planters would hang mistletoe and a Christmas stocking during the Christmas season," he went on, in a flight of eloquence. Even we Buddhists were moved by the spirit of the Christmas season!

Well, the temples are no more!

Was I imbued with the same gambling spirit of my forefathers and going for broke? This was a battle that was comprehensively lost. The dice was loaded against us! Was the spirit of the Suicide Club haunting me?

A BITTER BATTLE

THE DUNSINANE STRIKE

You never made a good planter till you went through a violent strike or faced an angry labour force.

No story of the plantations would be complete without reference to the conflicts that went on between the management and the work force. I am going to give you a story of one of the worst strikes in the history of the plantations in Ceylon.

The strike was on Dunsinane. Tony Fairweather was the Manager of the property. Plantation costs were rising and we had to make every attempt to bring them down. In an endeavour to do so, Fairweather, in consultation with me, brought down the rate payable for weeding contractors to Rs.5 per acre. We did this on the basis that a weeding contractor had an independent contract between him and the management, and we obtained a signed form from him stating that he would perform the work at Rs.5 per one acre of land. The form was signed voluntarily and the majority of the labour force fell in line with the scheme.

The Ceylon Workers' Congress was the main trade union on the plantation. This was Thondaman's home turf. A reduction in the weeding contract rates would have had a knock-on effect on the other plantations in the area. Thondaman was not going to allow this. We knew it was going to happen and, with some skilful manipulation, had half the work force on our side. When Thondaman called out a strike demanding the withdrawal of the independent contracts, we had half the work force disobeying Thondaman and agreeing to perform the work at the stipulated rate. This was where we made the first mistake, under-estimating Thondaman's power and influence within the plantations and in the political establishment of the day.

In order to understand the bitter conflict that ensued, it is necessary to study the makeup of the two protagonists on the opposing sides. Tony Fairweather, the Manager of Dunsinane, was a loner. He was 6'3" inches in height, had a very strong personality, was completely fearless and somewhat arrogant. He was an excellent planter who had enormous management skills. He also had a great knack for delegating authority. He backed up and supported his men to the hilt. Tony was totally uncompromising and looked down his nose at Thondaman. He was also of independent means and did not require a job to keep the wolf from the door.

Saumyamoorthy Thondaman was the best negotiator that this country has ever seen. He, too, was not inclined to step down in a confrontation. He would fight to the bitter end. He was the master at manipulating events and had the great ability to strike hard at the right time. The timing of his actions was his forté. The stage was thus set for a 'battle royale.'

Thondaman was also my friend and I warned Fairweather to approach this issue with some degree of caution. I cannot now recall how I was dragged in so intensely to oppose Thondaman, but that was exactly what I did. Tony asked me if I was going to support him all the way, to which I replied in the affirmative. For me there was no turning back. Tony was very fond of me and he had total confidence in me to stand with him and fight this to the end. He also realised that I had a great influence on the labour force and that I could keep a major part of the estate working, despite Thondaman's call for strike action. That was our strength.

That was also what enraged Thondaman, in that we broke up his union on his home turf and his biggest stronghold, Dunsinane. One hundred per cent of the workers on Dunsinane were members of the Ceylon Workers' Congress. I was able to reduce the membership to 50 per cent and, in place of the CWC, brought in the Illankai Tholilali Katchi (ITK). This was a Jaffna-based trade union and they were vying with Thondaman for a foothold on the plantations.

As it turned out, we had made an enormous mistake. Thondaman was going to fight us to the bitter end. A conference was scheduled to discuss the strike at the

Punduloya Planters' Club. The strike was in full swing, although we had taken its sting out as half the labour force was working. This was our strength and also what embittered Thondaman. He was now threatening a sub-district strike and if that did not force us to capitulate, he was going to pull out the Nuwara Eliya District and then call out an all-island strike.

"What the hell. Let him call out the whole island if he wants. We will still have Dunsinane working," Fairweather told me. I was extremely apprehensive of the developing situation and warned him that events could snowball out of control.

The district representatives of the CWC were going for the conference through Dunsinane. "Have all the workers plucking on the fields adjoining the roads so that they can see that the call for a strike has been a failure," said Fairweather. This action on our part was extremely provocative. I was very young and foolhardy. Nobody in his right mind would have taken on Thondaman in this manner. Thondaman had, in fact, asked a mutual friend, "Why is Herman doing this to me?" I could now not back out without betraying Tony. Was I imbued with the same gambling spirit of my forefathers and going for broke?

This was a battle that was comprehensively lost. The dice was loaded against us! Was the spirit of the Suicide Club haunting me?

Thondaman realised that this was a 'do or die' battle. If he did not succeed he would have lost more of his members to other trade unions on Dunsinane and also on the other estates in the area. This started the spiral of violence. The first victim of the strike was Nadarajah, a supervisor who was diligently carrying out our instructions. He was hacked to death with pruning knives.

The police officer in charge of the area was Sumith De Silva, a very close friend of mine. He had received intelligence reports that the CWC had instructed the strikers on Dunsinane and Sheen Group, the adjoining plantation,

to walk in to Dunsinane and chase out those who were working. One fine day, hordes of strikers, armed with clubs and sticks, were joined by other workers in the area and they descended on Dunsinane. They assaulted the non-strikers, who duly retaliated, and there was mayhem. We summoned the Punduloya police to quell the violence. When the police arrived, the labour force surrounded the police jeep and started pushing it down the hill. The sergeant in charge opened fire in the air and the strikers retreated, temporarily. Sumith realised that he would not be able to maintain law and order on the estate and brought reinforcements from Nuwara Eliya. One hundred and five policemen, fully armed with riot gear, tear gas and weapons, arrived on the estate. The wounded were housed at the Dunsinane hospital.

Thondaman then took the strike to the next level. "Go for Gunaratne and Fairweather," he instructed his members. Sumith once again contacted me and warned me of the developing situation. "Your life is now in danger and I will not be able to protect you," he stated. "I will have a covert operation team posted round your bungalow but there is no way I can do it 24/7. You had better settle this strike soon. I, too, am being pressurised from the government that I am assisting you in breaking the strike. You must realise that the politicians will ultimately succumb to pressure from Thondaman," he advised.

Sumith made it very clear to me that he would no longer be able to afford us personal protection. I had to obtain the services of an armed group from Colombo to guard my bungalow. These armed mercenary guys were good at controlling minor incidents in Colombo, but I quickly realised that they were completely out of their depth when nearly 1000 angry workers came at them with clubs and knives. I restricted their activities to the security of my bungalow.

I discussed this new situation with Fairweather. He was not prepared to relent. "Let's go down fighting," he said. I told him, however, that although the labour force was still partially working, we would not be able to protect them for much longer and it would be best that we settled it soon. "How are you going to do this?" he asked me. I told him that there was no other way to settle this strike other than to meet Thondaman and come to terms with him. He was not happy with this and told me so. The agents, too, were slowly applying pressure on him. In the meantime, I heard on the grapevine that Thondaman had contacted Sir John over the telephone in London and placed the full blame on Fairweather, adding that I was only carrying out Fairweather's instructions. Even at this juncture, Thondaman, my friend, was throwing me a lifeline! We had proved our point but the battle was decisively lost.

In the final days of the struggle, the strikers were demanding my removal from Dunsinane. In their

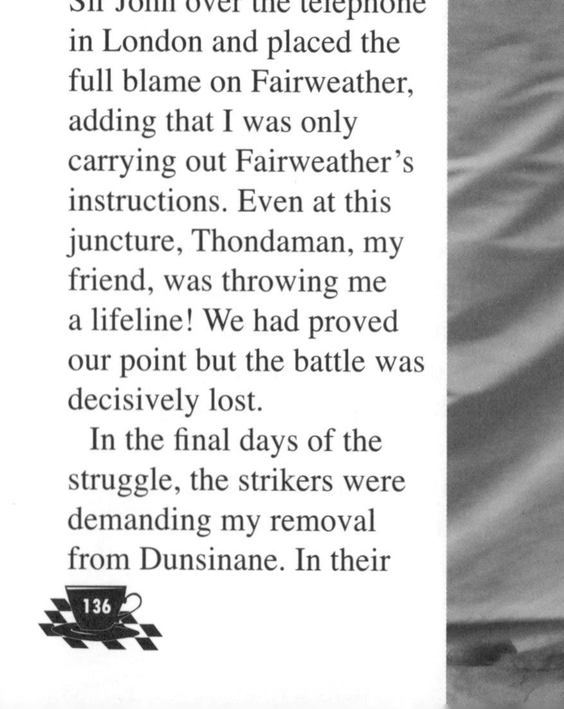

The day's tea toil
on a Salter scale

eyes it was not Fairweather but I who was responsible for this strike.

I decided to meet the trade union leader. His grand nephew was Radha Mathavan, who was one of my closest friends. He learnt the trade on Dunsinane, and was trained by me. I told Radha to find out where Thondaman was that weekend and resolved to meet him.

Radha phoned back and informed me that Thondaman was holidaying on his Meddegoda Estate in Udahentenna. We went to see him.

"Ah, my friend so you have come to see me." He hailed me as before, with not a trace of anger or irritation at this unannounced visit. He had a houseful of guests and introduced me to them. Not a word about the strike from this 'King Maker.' I called him to the side and broached the need for a settlement. "You know me well enough. Why did you wait so long to talk to me?" he said, showing disappointment at my not communicating with him. I apologised to him. He then invited me to stay behind for lunch and before I left, he told me, "Do not worry. We will summon a conference in Colombo and settle the strike," and that was that.

The conference was summoned in Colombo. We met briefly beforehand at the Galle Face Hotel and decided on the basis of the settlement. At the conference, after some sparring and an exchange of words the strike was settled. The demand for my removal was dropped, though it was the first item on the agenda. By this time Sir John Arbuthnot had been alerted by Thondaman and he visited the estate to find out exactly what had gone wrong. This was a very brief visit. In the report that he sent following his visit he stated that 'Mr. Gunaratne needs a change of scenery,' which was the British way of saying that I must leave Dunsinane. I was immediately transferred on promotion as Senior Assistant Superintendent of Ury Group, Passara. There was some bitterness and anger with me and the labour force was happy to see me go.

There is an interesting sequel to this story. Many years later, I suddenly received a telephone call from Mr. Gamini Salgado, the Director of George Steuart and Company. "Herman," he said, "a vacancy has arisen on Dunsinane Estate and it has been the unanimous decision of the Board that the job should be offered to you. It is one of our largest plantations and you will receive enhanced terms and conditions. Will you accept the position?" he queried. I jumped for joy at this honour, but realised that running Dunsinane would be very difficult for me after the long strike. "I am honoured that you have selected me for this job, but can you please give me about five days to make a decision?" I knew exactly what I was going to do.

I contacted my friend Saumyamoorthy Thondaman and told him that I would like to see him. Going to Dunsinane after all the trouble, without his blessings, was unthinkable. He was on Wavendon Estate on this occasion. He was happy, as usual, to see me. I told him that I was offered the job of Manager of Dunsinane and that I would only accept it if I had his support.

"What is the support you want from me? You take the job straight away. I will come with you in your car when you are going to take over. Do not worry. I will see that everything is OK," he declared. This was the quintessential Thondaman - a big man, larger than life. He congratulated me and accompanied me to Dunsinane when I went to take over. The labour saw me coming with the plantation messiah and they were more than surprised at this unusual happening. All he said was, "I have come with my friend to your estate on his first day. Give him all your support. We will both look after you."

There is a lesson for the aspiring planter. Never over-estimate your strength. Always negotiate. Never start something over which you do not have full control.

Thereafter I never had a strike on any of the plantations I worked on. I had learnt my lesson.

Silva was the Chief Dayaka (lay disciple) of the Buddhist temple. 'Thou shall not steal,' exhorted the Buddha. Silva not only stole but bought himself, with his stolen booty, the respectability of the Chief Lay Disciple at the temple. He was esteemed in the village for his piety and adherence to Buddhist principles

THEY TRIED TO SACK MY BOSS

'Gunaratne needs a change of scenery,' was Sir John Arbuthnot's comment (as stated earlier) when he visited Dunsinane after the strike. Dunsinane was a Sterling company and Ury Group, Passara, to which I was transferred belonged to a Rupee company called Nahavilla Estates Limited. This was perhaps a decline in status. There was some perceived sense of superiority when you worked for a Sterling company. To me it did not matter. I did some utterly unorthodox things on Dunsinane and the agents would have been completely justified in dealing with me more harshly. Thankfully this did not happen. It was merely a routine transfer.

Ury Group was in the Uva District of the island, in Passara. It was a sprawling plantation, extending from Badulla to the border of Passara. It consisted of five divisions, all managed by resident assistant superintendents. I was designated the Senior Assistant Superintendent, which was in fact a promotion. The Senior Assistant on Ury had to administer the whole plantation.

The Manager of Ury Group was J. R. Kunanayagam (Kunam), a very senior planter. Kunam came from a highly connected Jaffna Tamil family. He was a very genial man and we got on like a house on fire. He entrusted me with the responsibility of running the whole estate.

Kunam was under heavy fire from the Agents for poor performance on Ury. He confided in me that he was having a running battle with a director of George Steuart and Company called Roy Jonklaas (not his real name). Roy Jonklaas was a coarse character, quite unlike the other members of the Board of Directors. He had favourites, and he was overbearing and too heavy-handed in his dealings with the planters.

George Steuart and Company usually had very civilised, well-mannered men on the Board. Even when they sacked you, which they seldom did, you went out laughing and with no hard feelings. They gave you many chances if you were found

wanting in your work. It was considered the most prestigious agency house and all the planters clamoured to get into it. They also held the agency for the management of the best British companies.

Roy Jonklaas was like the new boy in the classroom. Abrasive, untouched by refinement and overbearing, I often wondered if the Board had taken leave of their senses to bring this man into the Board Room. He spoilt the delicate and urbane association that the company had with the planters. George Steuart and Company worked on one main management principle: the Superintendent or Manager is King. They always consulted you. They looked after you to the best of their ability. They supported you and never let you down, even when you made some mistakes. They did not take anonymous letters seriously. This was a pernicious problem on the plantations, with unsigned letters being addressed to the directors about every conceivable activity on the estate. If there was a ring of truth in the letters, they tactfully sent it to you under extreme 'Private and Confidential' cover. If the letters contained something factual, it was left to the Superintendent to take action to correct the situation. If the letters were about the Manager, you took notice of it anyway.

The anonymous letters to the agents were in addition to the spate of letters that the Manager, himself, received almost on a daily basis. I must confess, however, that some of these letters contained details of serious misdemeanours on the estate. I have been the recipient of anonymous letters upon which I have acted, of course with the greatest caution. Some of the letters, for instance, gave the details with clear directions of how tea thefts were taking place. One such letter resulted in the detection of one the biggest tea thefts from the Debedda Factory of Ury Group which had two tea factories. The Factory Officer was the culprit. We caught him red-handed one night, transporting some tea in a Morris Minor car belonging to an affluent village merchant. The affluence of the merchant

(Mudalali) was clearly due to the unabated thieving that he had engaged in for over 10 years. We made the tea, he simply stole it!

The planters of the entire Passara district had to pass his shop whenever they were going to the well known Uva Club. He knew the habits of every single planter. The time they left the plantation and the time they returned were all within his knowledge. It was almost as if he was mounting a close surveillance on the planters. Everyone knew that he was stealing tea. He was also very powerful in the area and the plantation executives were somewhat reluctant to deal with him, for fear of reprisals.

The informant told us, through an anonymous letter, that the tea was removed on the Uva Club Day when all of us went down to the club and did not return till around midnight. We were further told that there was nothing surreptitious about the tea thefts. The merchant, Silva *Mudalali* (not his real name), drove up to the Debedda Factory at around 9.30pm. The Factory Officer loaded the rear of the car from which all the seats were removed with tea, and Silva happily drove off. He unloaded the tea at his shop which was about 600 metres from the factory. It was as simple as that.

We were further told that he used to do this only once a week but lately he had been carrying out the theft twice a week.

When tea thefts of this magnitude took place it was a sure sign that the management had lost control of the property. This was indeed so. Stealing on a large scale was going on in every area. The culprits also happened to be quite powerful in the vicinity and could cause considerable problems for you, including bodily harm if you were not careful. The reader must know that all this arose as a result of Ury Group being surrounded by villages. The problems of thievery were not so serious in the homogeneous plantation belt on the Western side of the island (Nuwara Eliya area).

Harry Abeykoon was the other assistant of Ury Group on

Agratenna Division. We were great friends. I told Harry about the tea thefts and solicited his support to lay a trap for Silva *Mudalali*. Harry was one of those great characters in the planting fraternity. He was thoroughly reliable and completely loyal. He was also called Silent Harry, or Monosyllabic Harry. He used his words very carefully and did not waste his breath on one unnecessary word. Some even said that 'Harry opened his mouth only to drink.' That he did in fairly substantial quantities. The more he drank the more sober he was. He was that kind of man.

I received specific information that on Club Day which was a Wednesday, the theft would take place. I was also told that the Morris Minor car would arrive at the factory at any time between 9pm and 10pm. It would enter through the main gate and leave through the same gate. Harry and I deployed a reliable worker to maintain a watchful eye on this whole event. He was given a powerful torch, which he was instructed to flash in a particular way as soon as Silva *Mudalali* entered the factory. The transfer of tea from the factory to the car would take 10 minutes, we were told.

We positioned ourselves at the Wewessa Estate junction. We timed the short run from Wewessa to the Debedda factory, and it took exactly 10 minutes.

Harry and I commenced our vigil. As expected, our secret surveillance man flashed his torchlight and we advanced slowly towards the factory. The Morris Minor, with Silva *Mudalali* at the wheel was rolling out of the factory. We blocked the road in the estate Land Rover and pulled him out of the car. This normally taciturn and arrogant man was speechless and shivering like a leaf. Harry thumped him one or two blows on the frontal area of his forehead with a knuckle duster and we dragged him and the car back to the Debedda Factory. Silva *Mudalali* was the chief *Dayaka* (lay disciple) of the Buddhist temple. 'Thou shall not steal,' exhorted the Buddha. Silva *Mudalali* not only stole but bought himself with his stolen booty, the respectability of the Chief Lay Disciple at the temple. He was held in esteem in the village for his piety and adherence to Buddhist principles.

The Tea Maker, Godwin, appeared on the scene. He started shivering. I was mad with him and may have exercised my martial skills on him a little too vigorously when I was cautioned by Harry to leave him alone. We had now to inform the police and did not want to leave any visible injuries on the tea thieves. The stolen tea was weighed in the presence of the police, and it was around 500 kilos. Not a bad haul for half an hour's work. They were both handed over to the Passara Police.

This detection shook the whole of Ury Group. The staff and the labour now realised that we were quite serious in arresting the decline. Then came other bits and pieces of information, no longer through anonymous channels, as everyone now knew that neither Harry nor I would divulge the source of the information. The situation was bad. They were robbing the estate in a big way. We had a long way to go to combat other areas of theft.

Harry and I understood the extent of the decline. Tea was being robbed, green leaf was stolen, fertiliser was purloined and everybody was having a carnival at the expense of the property. Harry advised me to have a chat with the Old Man and tell him that the cleaning up operations had only started and that there was a long way to go. He told me, "Herman, be careful, we are now interfering with the lifestyles of the guys who are robbing the estate in a big way, and they are not going to take it lying down. You will have to get the Old Man's support and concurrence on everything that we are going to do." I agreed with Harry and resolved to talk to Kunam.

I had a frank discussion with Kunam and told him that the management controls seemed to have broken down everywhere. His reply was that he himself was insecure in his position and that he did not have the stomach to take on

the various miscreants as all this would have resulted in court cases and creating enemies in the area.

"Bloody Jonklaas himself is trying to sack me. How can I take on the whole of Ury Group? You and Harry should get on and do it. I will support you all the way." I could clearly understand the way that Kunam had felt.

"No, Sir, let's fix the problems on Ury and then Jonklaas will leave us alone," was my idea of the way to go. Kunam was willing to turn on the heat and go down this road. That was when Roy Jonklaas bowled his underarm ball.

There is a lesson here for the Colombo Agent. It is not possible for the Manager to perform at full capacity if he feels insecure and the Agent is gunning for him to eventually sack him. I realised that Kunam needed a strong back-up force to bolster his flagging morale. "Don't worry, Sir," I told him, "we will fix all the problems on Ury. Let me talk to the other assistants and we will sort out all these matters." I further asked him for independent authority to take action in all areas, without even reference to him. My only request was that if things got too hot, he must stand by us. Kunam readily agreed and seemed almost relieved that we were taking over the responsibility of bringing order to Ury. Roy Jonklaas was harassing him so much with letters and admonishments that he had to constantly run down to Colombo for legal advice and to get draft replies for the letters that he was receiving. He realised that Jonklaas was building up a case against him for dismissal and he was simply engaged in safeguarding his job. He had little time to run the estate. From Ury to Colombo was a seven-hour journey and Kunam had to do this at least twice a week. He took me fully into his confidence and asked me to help him. Both Harry and I had great affection for Kunam. We resolved not only to clean up the Augean stables but also to go all the way with Kunam in safeguarding his job.

This was when Roy Jonklaas did the unthinkable. He appointed the Factory Superintendent of Ury as a spy.

The spy came in the shape and size of his own brother, Peter Jonklaas. Peter's appointment had no precedent in the plantations system. He was given independent command of the Debedda Tea Factory. Kunam's Land Rover was taken over and given to Peter. This was a clear signal to the whole estate that Kunam was no longer in full control of the property. When this happened, loyalties were divided, and this was more so now that the staff and workers realised that the Colombo Director's own brother, Peter, was in independent control of the factory. Peter was not a diplomat. He gave the impression that his appointment was only temporary and that he would eventually be taking charge of the whole Group. This appointment broke Kunam's morale completely.

We began to wonder how George Steuart and Company, such a civilised and experienced Agency House, approved the appointment of Roy Jonklaas' own brother as a spy. By this time, the blustering Jonklaas had convinced the Board of Directors that he had all the answers to the problems of plantations not faring too well. The story reached us on the grapevine that some senior Directors of the company were not too happy about this appointment as well as the actions of the 'new boy in the classroom,' Roy Jonklaas.

Peter was quite friendly with me and Harry. Kunam became quite nervous wondering if we were going to switch our loyalties. I could gather this from the discussions that he had with me after Peter's appointment. Harry and I decided to address this problem directly with Kunam. We sought an appointment with him to deal with this matter. He invited us to dinner at the Ury big bungalow. We told him in the clearest possible terms, that as far as we were concerned he was our boss and that we would sail with him all the way. He was relieved and appeared grateful.

Peter, in the meantime, was delving not only into matters concerning the factory but into other areas that did not come under his purview. He could not proceed further in this direction as nothing was forthcoming from us. We instructed our staff to keep aloof from Peter and not to divulge any information to him.

He invited both Harry and me to dinner and tried to smooth talk us into throwing our lot in with him. "George Steuart and Company thinks very highly of the two of you. You will soon be up for a very good promotion, and you must help me to get Ury going. You must know on which side your bread is buttered." We detested him, not for what he said, but because he thought that we would betray our boss for a mess of pottage.

We told him clearly that as far as we were concerned we served only the Manager of Ury Group, and that was Mr. Kunanayagam - nothing more, nothing less. If he wanted any information, support, or assistance from us, he would have to come through Kunam. We added that we would be acting only on the directives of Kunam and no one else. I must say, in fairness to Peter, that our stance and attitude did not alter his friendship and association with us. He may even have had greater respect for us.

By this time we were cracking down on the thefts and corruption within the group, albeit somewhat more slowly, because of this new appointment. We now had a whole lot of forces working against us, including those at the receiving end of our investigations, as well as Peter Jonklaas himself and the doubled-up spate of anonymous letters now being received and read by Roy in the Head Office in Colombo, who seemed to know exactly what was going on.

Peter, too, was making his 'contribution' and I think he told his brother, Roy, that he was not receiving any cooperation from us.

They decided to go down another road.

A little about Kunam's family at this point as it is essential for my story. Kunam came from one of the high class families in Jaffna. He was married to a tall, attractive lady, Wimala, also from Jaffna. Wimala had very close connections to a leading Tamil family in the country. Her brother, Mahes Kunaratnam, was the General Manager of Cargills, Ceylon's leading department store in that era. Rear Admiral Rajan Kadiragamar, the Commander of the Ceylon Navy, was married to Wimala's sister. Sam Kadiragamar QC, was Rajan's brother. Lakshman Kadiragamar was the other brother, a President's Counsel and a leading lawyer at that time. They were some of the most accomplished men in the country. They were fiercely independent, very wealthy, highly sophisticated and very, very straightforward. To sit and talk to them about matters of the world were some of my most enjoyable and stimulating experiences. Famous legal battles and the stories of naval exploits were among the stories that the Kadiragamars shared with us.

Kunam also laid it on thick. He used to invite the Directors of George Steuart and Company to Trincomalee in the East for the holidays. They were wined and dined in style at Naval House, the Commander's official residence, where the naval orchestra played light music over five-course dinners. Special trips were organised by the Navy Commander in the gun boats for the Directors. Rear Admiral Rajan dazzled them with naval honours and ceremony. One senior Director was even given the honour of inspecting the naval Guard of Honour.

This, the reader will understand, is a rare honour for visitors. They came away from Trincomalee completely dazzled and impressed with Kunam's hospitality. After all, it was for Kunam that the Navy Commander was laying all this on.

I, too, had the privilege of being Kunam's guest at Trincomalee. The Rear Admiral, knowing full well that I was Kunam's friend at a difficult time, turned on the show for me too. Naval House was the residence of Mountbatten of Burma, the Admiral of the Fleet, and also of Sir Geoffrey Leighton, Naval Commander of Ceylon. It was magnificently furnished. You were transported into another world of naval pomp and pageantry. Life was good to us. I slowly whispered to Kunam, "Sir, we may have done some merit in our previous birth to sit in Lord Louis Mountbatten's bungalow and drink champagne at sunset with the Commander of the Navy." Kunam took all this in his stride. "Knock the drinks down, Herman, and have a good time when it is offered to us," he quipped.

The Kadiragamars were frequent visitors to the Ury bungalow. On every occasion when they came, Kunam and Wimala invited me to dinner. It was their way of thanking me for the loyalty and friendship that I gave them. I was going to use this association to Kunam's full advantage. But that was later. It was Sam Kadiragamar who was replying to all the letters that Kunam got from the agents. Sam turned the whole thing round on Jonklaas and stated that Kunam was being persecuted as Jonklaas was doing everything within his power to appoint his brother to the prestigious position of the Manager of Ury.

In the meantime, Peter Jonklaas was collecting all the information of what was going wrong on Ury. He was also surreptitiously feeding this information to his big brother. He discovered our Achilles Heel. The tea bushes on any plantation in the world must be plucked every seven days. If you do not do this, the green leaf that comes into the factory is too coarse for the manufacture and production of good tea. On Ury we had a huge problem with the labour. Their reporting to work on the estate was erratic and they went to the village instead, since they were paid more money there. We could never get the plucking rounds in order. This was a massive problem. We were doing everything to address the problem by offering incentives, by gently arm-twisting the labour, and by stopping rations for those not turning up for work, issuing them letters of warning and using all the means at our disposal to encourage better attendance.

The plucking rounds, however, were far from satisfactory. Peter was examining the chart at the factory and questioned us about the elongated rounds. We had three divisions of Ury Group near Passara town. Instead of plucking every seven days, the round extended to 15 days on these divisions. Lucrative work was available in the town and the labour chose to take the opportunity to earn more. The plucking rounds in the factory were maintained in a large book. We heard that Peter was pouring over this book with undue interest.

I realised that this would be brought to the notice of the Colombo office. We could quite easily have given excuses for these situations but in the plantation system, excuses are of no value and are seldom accepted. Peter was then seen copying down the tea book with the elongated rounds on a large sheet of paper. This was too big and laborious a job for him. He delegated an Assistant Factory Officer to complete the task. This man was from my village in Ruhuna and he told me that Peter Jonklaas was collecting information on the extended rounds.

We were suddenly informed that John Davis, the Manager of Glen Alpin Group and the Visiting Agent of Ury, would be paying a surprise and unscheduled visit to the property. They were turning the heat on. I realised that the plucking rounds would be the main area of scrutiny. John Davis was a senior planter and he was not a participant in the persecution. He was going to report on the facts, which were weighed against us. Kunam and Davis had the same planting experience. I told Kunam that we should try to brazen it out with Davis, saying that the growth was slow on the outlying divisions and that was the reason for the delayed rounds. All very lame excuses, no doubt, but some explanation had to be given.

Davis came to the estate. As expected he went round and saw the leaves waving in the air as a result of the delayed rounds. Peter took him to the factory and showed him the plucking charts. We realised that Davis would send a very unfavourable report to the agents. We knew that this would be followed by a

This is where we caught Silva Mudalali stealing the tea

visit from Roy Jonklaas. The drama played out exactly as we had anticipated.

A week later we were informed that not Jonklaas but Gamini Salgado, a very senior director of the company would be visiting the plantation. Jonklaas had ducked the issue as by this time, Sam Kadirgamar had informed the Board that there was a clear case of persecution of Kunam by Jonklaas.

Gamini Salgado was one of the most respected members in our profession. He was a planter who went on to become a Director of George Steuart and Company. A gentleman to his fingertips, there was no way in which he was going to participate in anything improper or unethical. Gamini was an accomplished sportsman, and an excellent cricketer who scored a century at the Royal-Thomian match (the Eton and Harrow of Ceylon). This century is still talked about in cricketing circles. He also played rugby for Royal. A tall man with an imposing personality, very polished and soft spoken, Gamini would only play by the Queensberry Rules. Of this, we were sure. Gamini's winning rugby team also included Rear Admiral Rajan Kadiragamar who scrummed down with him. Rajan and Gamini were close personal friends, as only those playing in the same rugby team can be.

The only 'fly in the ointment' would be the plucking rounds book in the factory. We could brazen most things out but in the face of hard evidence derived from this book, there was little we could do. I mentioned these apprehensions to Harry. He realised the importance of what I was saying. "Harry, if the book went missing then I think we could bluff our way through this problem." "Give me a few days, and I will see what I can do," was all he said.

Two days before Gamini arrived on the property Harry invited me to dinner at his Agratenna Bungalow. The offending book was lying innocently on his sofa. He glanced at it and looked at me. No words - just the book on the sofa and a triumphant gleam in his eye. I knew better than to ask him the details. "It is better burnt," was all I said. We decided that Kunam should know nothing about the purloined book. That way he could genuinely express surprise and disbelief.

When Kunam told me of Gamini's visit, I knew exactly how we should handle the affair. Kunam was not in the mood to think this through. I told him, "Sir, let's get the Rear Admiral and Sam Kadiragamar to be present at the bungalow when Gamini arrives." Gamini would be reluctant to read the riot act to us with the Rear Admiral and Sam Kadiragamar present. I knew that Gamini had very strong 'old boy' ties and that he was not going to embarrass his rugby playing colleague by dealing too harshly with us in the presence of Rear Admiral Kadiragamar and Queen's Counsel Sam Kadiragamar. Kunam jumped at the idea. Of course, I suggested that we should make it appear as if the Kadiragamars were spending a few days on Ury, and had not come up for the visit of Gamini Salgado. Kunam's family was very united and they would do anything for him. The Kadiragamars arrived the day before Gamini's visit and settled down at the bungalow.

On the day of Gamini's arrival, Kunam instructed me to be present at the estate office and to bring Harry along. The office was just a few yards away from the bungalow. We took positions in the office and waited anxiously for Kunam.

When Gamini arrived, he saw his old friends at the bungalow and did not speak a word about what he had come up to do. They had a couple of drinks and a sumptuous lunch and Gamini, as anticipated, told Kunam, "Let's get down to the office and discuss a few matters."

In the meantime, Peter Jonklaas was raising Cain at the factory looking for the missing plucking round charts. He was tearing his hair out, and raving and ranting at the factory staff. We had removed the main plank of evidence against us.

Gamini arrived at the office. Suave and impeccably turned out, he was the very embodiment of refinement. We were introduced to him. After a few pleasantries, he asked me for the plucking rounds chart. I telephoned the factory where Peter Jonklaas was doing a

last desperate search for the missing book.

"Peter," I said with a dead pan expression, "Mr. Gamini Salgado wants you to send the plucking rounds book to the office immediately."

"I can't send the bloody book because I can't find it," he rasped.

I relayed this information to the Director. If he was surprised, he did not show it. Kunam could not suppress his relief at the missing book. Gamini then went on to say that John Davis had examined the book and found a very unsatisfactory state of affairs with regard to the maintenance of the plucking rounds. I then intervened and told the visitor that although the plucking rounds were elongated on some divisions, we had brought it into order and that if the book was available, the Director would see this for himself. I told him further that the missing book was in the custody Peter Jonklaas and it was he who was running around with it. The fact that it was missing was very strange and significant. We turned the whole episode of the missing book to our advantage.

Gamini Salgado realised that all of us were standing firmly behind Kunam. He may even have admired the stand that we were taking. He would never have been a party to any 'fixing' operation like his colleague, Roy. It was inconceivable for him to play the game other than by the rules. He left us after asking us to sort the problems of the plucking rounds as soon as possible.

Upon his return to Colombo, George Steuart and Company had also realised that letting Roy Jonklaas lose was damaging the reputation of the company.

Kunam was transferred to Noragalla Estate, Uda Karawita, after a reasonable period of time. He was taken out of the clutches of Roy Jonklaas. Roy's brother, too, was immediately transferred from Ury. The problem was resolved in the normal civilised fashion adopted by George Steuart and Company. Gamini was the 'rapier.' Jonklaas was the 'bludgeon,' leaving a trail of blood.

All this, of course, was
too complicated for Ana
but he memorised these
instructions. He devised the
acronym, S W H N A:

S – serviette
W – water
H – watch host
N – no noise
A – armpits 50 cent coin

DINNER WITH THE MOSSOPS

Wining and dining properly was an essential part of the training a planter has to undergo. It was also a nightmare for the uninitiated. Table manners, table craft, the use of the array of cutlery and crockery, knives, forks, soup spoons and dessert spoons had to be done the right way. The only 'right way' was the way the British did it. Most of the young planters had to go through this torture. Since it was a part of the culture one had to do it with elegance to gain ultimate acceptance. I, for one, did not take this too seriously and was never afraid to ask my host how to handle a particular piece of 'weaponry.' When wines were served it was customary for the host to ask you if the wine was too sweet or too dry. I simply answered that I did not know one wine from another. If it tasted good, that was good enough for me. To my mind, this was far better than pretending to be a wine connoisseur, when everybody around you knew very clearly that you were not. To pretend was too tiring for me and it was something I could not bother too much about.

This story is about how a colleague of mine handled his first dinner. He had the sense of humour to laugh about it himself. I will relate the story, not only as told to me but as repeated many times at planters' gatherings.

Ana Jayasekera (he is still very much at large) was one of those remarkable characters in the Plantation Raj. He was a product of Ananda College, Colombo. This was a very rare occurrence because most plantation recruits were from the three leading schools in the island: St. Thomas' College, Mount Lavinia; Royal College, Colombo and Trinity College, Kandy. Trinity swept the board having been the nursery for plantation recruits. There was some good-natured banter and snobbery when an Anandian was about. 'Did you go for the interview in a sarong? Have they made a mistake and appointed you as an SD? Are you sure you were not appointed as a Kanakapulle?' When an Anandian spoke about having played cricket, he was asked whether he played in a paddy field with a tennis ball and with his sarong tucked up with his what-you-may-call-them dangling in the air. Ana Jayasekera gave as good as he got. 'We Anandians are not like you spineless scum who ape the white man. We are good Sinhala Buddhist products who have our feet on *terra firma*. Our colours are maroon and gol,' he said ('gol' meaning gold since some of them had a pronunciation problem, and complexes to boot). Not Ana though. He did not have any complexes and was eventually accepted as a fully-fledged member of the Raj. The barbs, sometimes cruel but mostly in jest, were taken by him in good spirit. Ana seemed to batten on the barbs. This is the story of his first dinner with his new boss, Chris Mossop, on Mocha Estate, Maskeliya.

He recalls: 'I took over Mocha Estate as the Assistant Superintendent and was invited for dinner by the Mossops. You know, we Ananda College boys have never used a spoon and fork in our lives and I was wondering how to tackle this first dinner. What the hell, I thought, and decided to do whatever the Mossops did.' He continued:

'My more experienced colleagues, who have gone through the ordeal and were masters at the art, went on to tell me, "When the food is placed on the table, do not grab whatever is served, as you would do at home. Fumble with the serviette, drink a glass of water, nonchalantly. Watch your host. Don't stare at his hands but furtively observe what piece of cutlery he takes up from the array of 'weapons' placed on the left and right side of the table. Do the same. Don't make a big noise with the clank of the knives and forks on the plate. Don't throw your arms about. You must tackle the food as if you had a 50 cent coin under your armpits and you had to go through the meal with the coin in place. Take only small mouthfuls of the food. Do not stuff your mouth with big pieces of fish or meat.' All this, of course, was too complicated for Ana but he memorised these instructions. He devised the acronym, S W H N A:

S - serviette

W - water

H - watch host

N - no noise

A - armpits 50 cent coin

It was difficult for him to remember all the dining instructions. He therefore kept repeating this check list to himself and mentally ticked them off as he passed them one by one.

Ana continued: 'The Mossops greeted me warmly and asked me what I would like to drink. I plunged for the safety of a beer, having been warned by colleagues not go for anything stronger. This bloody Mossop plonked a huge tankard in front of me and poured almost a bottle of beer into it. I gulped it down. He poured another bottle. I gulped that down too. When the third bottle was poured I was quite tipsy. My bladder was full (in Sinhala this is far more pithy and colourful). I did not know what to do. I was scared to stand up in case I wet my pants. I started sweating and could hardly talk with an enlarged bladder. The dinner bell was rung and Mossop invited me to the dining room. Mossop, perhaps sensing my discomfiture, said, "Jayasekera, would you like to wash your hands?" Who the hell knows what that means? I looked at my hands and said, "No, my hands are OK" Why could the b----r not have said, "Do you want to use the toilet?" How the f--k do I know that 'washing the hands' means the same thing?'

The euphemisms and the parlour room courtesies were lost on Ana. Ana was at his vintage best, and he used to relate this story in the presence of all the European planters who were in fits of laughter when he finished with his travails at dinner.

'Then came the bloody dinner. I could hardly walk to the dining table for fear that I would lose control of my bladder. I was cursing the bloody Mossops for putting me through this agony. The tables were all laid in the finest chinaware, and cut crystalware glasses were placed for water. If the food was going to be as elaborate as the table dressings, I was in for a good dinner, I thought.'

Ana went on: 'First it was a bloody starter. Who the hell knows what a starter is? Thankfully everything was first served to the Mossop woman and I did exactly what she did. While

Tea tasting

partaking of this fare I was furtively looking at my pants to see whether they were wet. So far, so good. At home, the domestics place string hoppers and curries and we go for it with our fingers. That was a far cry from the weaponry of the Mossops. A serviette was placed on my lap by the butler. What damn serviette for me, we go for dinner and wipe our hands on the table cloth! Then came the soup. Bloody hell, I could not take any more liquids into my system with three bottles of beer sitting inside me. Next was the fish course. This was an absolute disaster. The Butler brought three pieces of fish. Each slice of fish was the size of a 10 rupee note. Mrs. Mossop was served. She took one piece onto her plate. It was then served to me. I could never imagine that one person was supposed to take only a small piece of fish. In our houses, even if there are only two guests, there are about 10 pieces (this by the way, reader, is true). Straight away I grabbed the two remaining pieces onto my plate. There was an uncomfortable hush. The butler looked completely flustered. Mrs. Mossop was rolling her eyeballs and looking at Chris Mossop, and the unspoken words were perhaps, *From which woodwork did this specimen creep out?* The butler was gravitating in confusion between Mr. Mossop and Mrs. Mossop. Mossop finally said, "No darling, I won't have the fish." Anyway, there was no bloody fish for Mossop to have. I had grabbed both pieces onto my plate.'

Ana had put paid to Mossop's piece of fish! He then realised that he had screwed up the fish course. He was looking like the village bumpkin who had swallowed a golf ball. No fish for Mossop, bladder at bursting point, and there was a lull in the conversation. Ana was hoping that the ground would open up and swallow him. He soldiered on.

Then, Ana says, came the beef course. He was not going to attack the beef course the same way he had the fish. When he was served, he made sure that he took only a tiny piece of beef but filled up his plate with potatoes, tomatoes and onions.

Mossop did not have to go without his beef with a thoroughly restrained Jayasekera. He had looked at Ana in relief for leaving some for him. Mrs. Mossop was relieved that the new assistant was considerate with the beef course!

Ana Jayasekera, continuing his narration, said, 'The bloody knives were blunt and when I tried to cut an onion it jumped out of my plate and ended up on the Mossop woman's lap.' Both Mossops were now rolling their eyeballs. Mrs. Mossop had gingerly taken the onion and placed it on her side plate. Ana had one onion less! He had scored a bull's eye!

Ana went on to say, 'Can you imagine my position? The disaster of the fish course and the beef course was nothing compared to me, just about to piss in my pants. In addition to all this I was in a bath of perspiration and Mrs. Mossop did not help the situation. She kept on asking me if I was well and whether I wanted to rest in one of their rooms. Bloody hell, the Mossops and the dinners were coming out of my ears. I wanted to flee from the bungalow as soon as possible.'

The dessert had passed uneventfully. Ana had rushed out of the bungalow and watered the Mossop roses generously before retreating to his bungalow. 'The relief of pissing into Mossop's roses cannot be described. It was the nearest thing to heaven for me,' Ana said, to roars of laughter.

There is a lesson somewhere for the aspiring planter and for the British boss. All of us went through this nightmare with varying degrees of embarrassment. I, thereafter, made sure that all those who crept under me were given a rudimentary training in table craft. The British euphemisms like 'washing your hands,' 'powdering your nose,' and 'going round the corner' were explained very clearly to the novices.

Ana Jayasekera was not put off by these events and he was able to laugh at himself. He kept all of us regaled with these stories. But more was to come.

The two teasers - they outwitted the master seducers comprehensively

TWO LOVELY GIRLS AND THE GATEKEEPER AT WATTAGODDE

Two friends of mine visited me on Dunsinane, and on the way back to their own bungalow at Somerset Estate, Radella, they had a strange and unique experience. I will call my friends Tony and Larry (not their real names). We had a lunch party on Dunsinane, where liquor flowed freely and the sumptuous lunch served was enjoyed by all. They left Dunsinane reluctantly, as they had to supervise the night manufacture but we continued with the party until late evening. We tried our best to get them to stay behind without breaking up the party but the conscientious planters refused, telling us, "Work comes first. You guys carry on."

To reach Somerset they had to take the road from Dunsinane through Talawakelle to Radella. There is a road through Wattagodde Estate called the Wattagodde short cut which reduces travelling time by about 30 minutes. Only planters known to the Manager were allowed to use this roadway as it had to pass close to the tea factory and permitting outsiders to use this road would encourage tea thefts. However, they were hard pressed to prevent non-planters from using it. The management then gave the names of the planters in the area to a gatekeeper who was installed to prevent unauthorised vehicles. The gatekeeper grandly guarded a book, in which he was instructed to take down the names and signatures of those authorised to use the road.

The gatekeeper did not know a word of English and as far as he was concerned, anyone signing the book in English could drive through. Tony and Larry were not from the area and the gatekeeper did not know them. He proffered the pass book in which they had to write their names and addresses. Not knowing what this was all about they asked the gatekeeper what the reason for the book was. *'Oppum podunga,'* they were told. *'Dorai kalaile postum papara.'* ('Sign the book. The Manager looks at it in the morning.')

Tony and Larry were going to have some fun at the

Manager's expense. They took out their pens and with a flourish signed:

Winston Churchill - England

Aga Khan - God knows where

The gatekeeper looked knowingly at the book and lifted the barrier to allow them to pass.

The Manager perused the book the next morning and summoned the gatekeeper. "You bloody fool! Why did you let them pass? Who were they?" he berated. The poor man pleaded ignorance of the English language and begged of the Manager to appoint another gatekeeper. Tony and Larry later related this incident down at the club. All the others who passed through used similar names on the visitors' book:

Charlie Chaplin

Che Guevara

Alexander the Great

The book was withdrawn and the gate was permanently closed!

Passing through Talawakelle, they saw two pretty English girls with backpacks at the bus stop. They were casting covetous glances at all the passers-by, in the hope of thumbing a ride to Nuwara Eliya for the night.

Larry smacked his lips and asked Tony, 'Shall we try our luck?'

This was grist to Tony's mill.

'Why not,' he reacted with eager enthusiasm.

Larry was a charmer. He gallantly got out of the car with his toothpaste smile and said to the girls, 'Can we give you a ride? Where are you heading to?'

'To Nuwara Eliya' the girls replied.

A master at picking up foreign girls, Larry continued, 'We are two planters also going to Nuwara Eliya. Get in and we will give you a lift.'

In one smooth, elegant move he opened the door and helped them inside before they could refuse. It is not easy,

SUPERINTENDENT's
BUNGALOW
CIRCUIT
BUNGALOW

this coordinated pick up. If you fumble you have lost it. Larry and Tony were the up-country 'artistes' at this game. They were often the envy of many at the Golf Club when they suddenly appeared, as they do, with gorgeous girls. The night manufacture, their reason for the early departure from Dunsinane, was forgotten!

The introductions were made.

'I am Larry, the Manager of Somerset Estate, and this is Tony, my friend from Tangakelle Estate. These are the largest plantations in Nuwara Eliya,' they told the girls, liberally inflating the size of their plantations.

The girls demurely introduced themselves.

'This is Jennifer and I am Anne,' said the strong, tough-looking girl.

They were both dressed in figure-hugging shorts, giving a good display of their shapely legs. Jennifer was the gentle one, and it was Anne who was doing the talking, with Jennifer going along for the ride. They were both quite flirtatious and coquettish. Larry and Tony now warmed up to the anticipated activities of the night and they started laying it on thick. They were both Burgher planters and communicated between themselves in Sinhala.

'You take Jennifer,' Larry instructed Tony. 'I will handle Anne.'

Larry was the tough guy and he was taking on the strong Anne as his companion for the night. Larry was having fantasies of a lascivious night rolling on the bed, with Anne dealing blow for blow. All these exchanges were going on in Sinhala. They were pretending they were talking about the estate as it would otherwise have seemed rude to be communicating in a different language when everybody around spoke English. Tony reconciled himself to a night with the gentle Jennifer. They were both to retire to the Somerset Bungalow. Larry was the Manager of Somerset, and they had to pass the estate's bungalow on the way to Nuwara Eliya.

Tony pointed out the luxurious bungalow to the girls and they gasped with delight.

Larry and Tony had not yet sprung the invitation for the night, but they had worked out the strategy. 'Let's take them to the Golf Club to soften them up with a few drinks and then make the proposal for the night,' was the decision they arrived at.

They had decided on the different bedrooms that were going to be offered to the two girls. The rooms were to be far apart, in anticipation of vigorous and lively lovemaking.

When they arrived at the Golf Club, Larry and Tony told the girls to keep their backpacks in the car. They were not going to leave any evidence of the pick up at Talawakelle. The members at the club nearly jumped out of their skin when they saw the two girls with the planters.

They too broke into Sinhala.

'You lucky bastards! Where are these girls from?' they asked enviously.

'They are our friends,' was the non-committal reply.

Everybody started plying them with drinks, as it usually happens when you walked in with girls. With more than a few drinks inside them, Larry and Tony got more and more adventurous. A little touch, a little rub of the shoulders, were all part of the foreplay. The girls responded, if not with alacrity, but with nonchalance. They were the ultimate teasers. Tony and Larry were set for the night.

They called the girls aside, out of the earshot of the others, and said, 'It is now too late for you to find accommodation in Nuwara Eliya. You are welcome to stay with us tonight.'

They agreed at once. As far as Tony and Larry were concerned, the girls were now in bed and they had only to take the panties off! Anticipation rose high. They telephoned the Somerset bungalow and told the cook to make a three-course meal. A few bottles of wine were collected from the club and they made their way to the bungalow. A candlelit three-course dinner with wine was the arrangement for the night. The ideal

recipe for seduction.

The nitty gritties were now being now worked. 'As we arrive at the bungalow, we will ask the girls to freshen up with a hot water bath and a change of clothes. We ourselves will dress up for dinner.' They were going to seduce Anne and Jennifer in style.

'Get them into two separate rooms!' Tony instructed Larry. Somerset had four bedrooms.

They arrived at the Somerset bungalow around 9pm and immediately set to work. The two girls were shown the two rooms. However, they opted to retire to the same room, stating that they would take the separate rooms after they freshened up. The cook had set the table up for the night of seduction. It was candlelit with vases of colourful flowers adorning it. The cook was used to these nights and was obviously quite familiar with Larry's *modus operandi*.

The two planters retired to their respective bedrooms and reappeared a little while later. They were dressed for the kill. Tony was in one of Larry's shirts and Larry was in a coat and tie. Tony had not brought his clothes along, as this lottery of the two girls was quite unexpected. He had come ready only to visit me on Dunsinane for lunch.

The drinks trolley was laden with all types of liquor. Black Label whisky, imported beer, Campari and the wines brought from the Golf Club. The girls appeared a little later. The planters had fixed themselves two strong Johnny Walker Black Label whiskies. Anne was attired in a pair of tight-fitting jeans. Jennifer wore a delicate frock with some floral design. She had looked absolutely smashing. Anne was good-looking too but she had worn her hair tied up at the back, and it was as if she was dressing down for the occasion.

The girls opted for a glass of red Beaujolais wine. Larry and Tony were going for double whiskies. They were getting themselves in the mood for a night of serious lovemaking.

They invited the girls to share another bottle of wine but they were sipping the wine slowly. Larry, the master at seduction, casually got up from his seat on the pretext of checking on the food and returned to take a seat beside Anne, his choice for the night. He edged closer and closer to her and ultimately placed his arm round her shoulder. Anne carried on with the evening, not rejecting the closeness but with little or no reciprocation. Larry thought this was because Tony had not made any move on Jennifer and that Anne was therefore showing some reluctance.

He told his friend in muttered Sinhala, 'You bloody fool, make your move soon on the other one.' Tony lacked the finesse of his friend and was drumming up the courage to make his move with another drink. The atmosphere was a little tense since the progress was slow. Their seductions in the past had worked far more smoothly, with kisses and embraces and walking arm in arm to the garden for more intimate moments.

Tony then plucked up the courage and invited Jennifer to see the garden. Anne, however, intervened and told the two planters, 'We have had a long day. Let us go to sleep early.'

Larry told his friend in Sinhala again, 'They want to get down to business fast. Let's order the dinner and then start on them.'

The dinner gong was sounded and the foursome moved to the dining room. Barely had the food been placed on the table before the girls started attacking the meal ravenously. Again in Sinhala, Tony whispered under his breath, 'These two seem to be starving.' Anne and Jennifer did not leave a morsel of food uneaten, and they not only ate the food but also finished the hot bread rolls. They seemed not to have had anything to eat for a long time.

When the dessert of chocolate soufflé arrived, double helpings were taken by the girls. The dinner was finally over. The girls told the two friends who were now with heightened expectations, 'We will change for the night and

go to the separate rooms. Give us a little time.' They retired to the same bedroom.

Tony and Larry leapt into their rooms, got into sarongs and came back to the sitting room to await the arrival of the girls for the business of the night. They were not going to waste time removing cumbersome trousers and shirts. They poured themselves two more drinks, and waited and waited and waited. No girls appeared. The planters concluded that the girls must have been tired and decided to give them some more time. One hour passed, and still no girls. By this time the liquor was taking effect and the men were getting irritated.

The language changed and was no more polite and suave. 'Where the f--k are they? What the bloody hell are they doing for so long, changing their bloody clothes?' The two friends were now getting angry since the night of lovemaking was receding before them. Still they harboured some hope that the tired girls would return to their arms. More waiting. But no girls.

Every planter's bungalow has a discreetly placed night lamp in the bedroom. The lamp is very dim and hardly scatters any light. There is also a fan light in every room. Larry was the well-built guy, whereas Tony was a short, thin lightweight. Larry had a plan.

'I will bring a chair,' he told his frustrated friend. 'You are lighter than me. Stand up on the chair and see what the bloody hell is going on.'

Tony agreed. A chair was brought and Tony slowly climbed on it and peered through the fanlight. It took him a little time to get accustomed to the very dim light from the night lamp. He noticed no movement in the room. There was silence.

He then peered eagerly at the bed. He saw Anne and Jennifer fast asleep in each other's arms and nearly fell off the chair.

'Two f---ing lesbians!'

The two friends were caught hook, line and sinker.

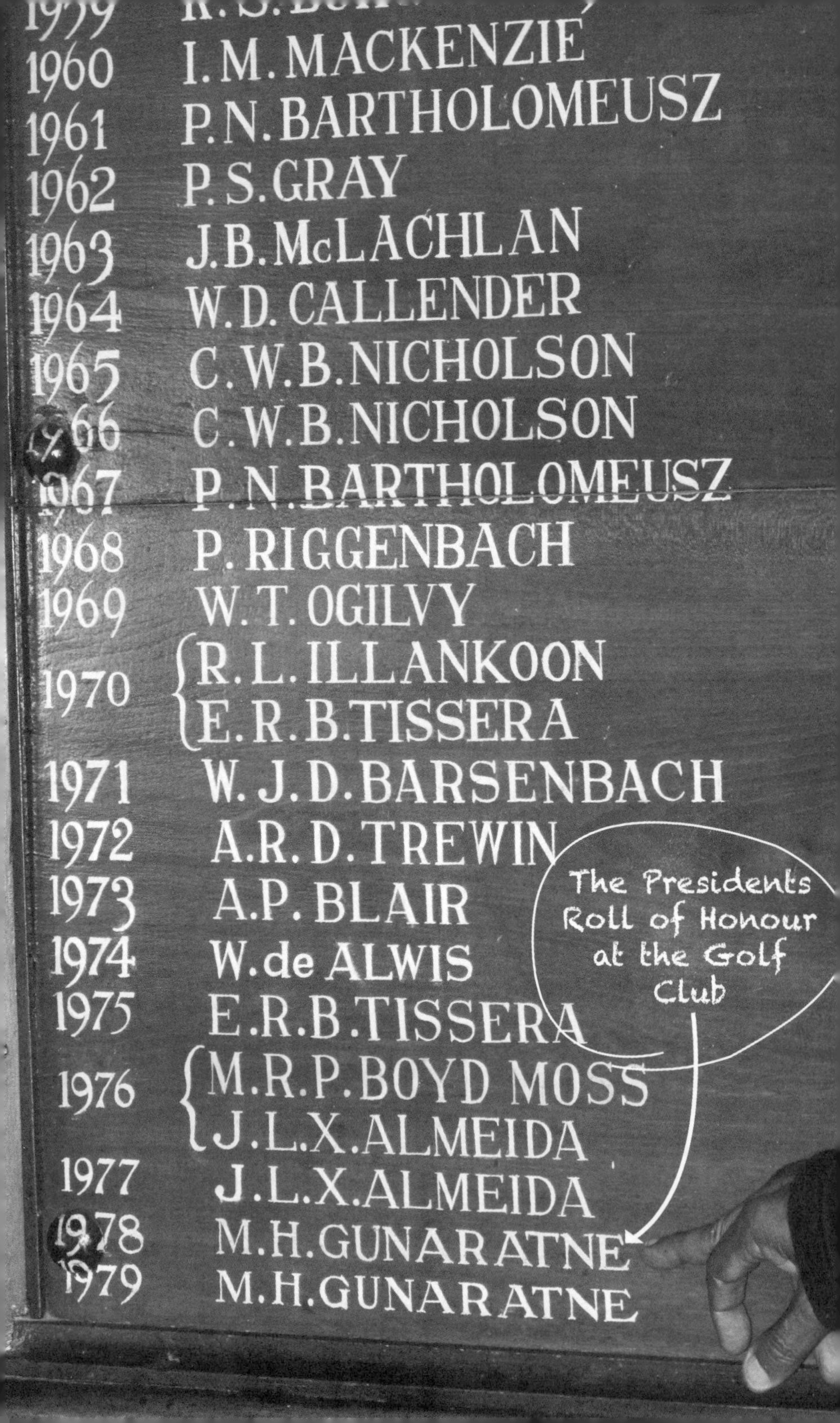

1960	I. M. MACKENZIE
1961	P. N. BARTHOLOMEUSZ
1962	P. S. GRAY
1963	J. B. McLACHLAN
1964	W. D. CALLENDER
1965	C. W. B. NICHOLSON
1966	C. W. B. NICHOLSON
1967	P. N. BARTHOLOMEUSZ
1968	P. RIGGENBACH
1969	W. T. OGILVY
1970	R. L. ILLANKOON E. R. B. TISSERA
1971	W. J. D. BARSENBACH
1972	A. R. D. TREWIN
1973	A. P. BLAIR
1974	W. de ALWIS
1975	E. R. B. TISSERA
1976	M. R. P. BOYD MOSS J. L. X. ALMEIDA
1977	J. L. X. ALMEIDA
1978	M. H. GUNARATNE
1979	M. H. GUNARATNE

The Presidents Roll of Honour at the Golf Club

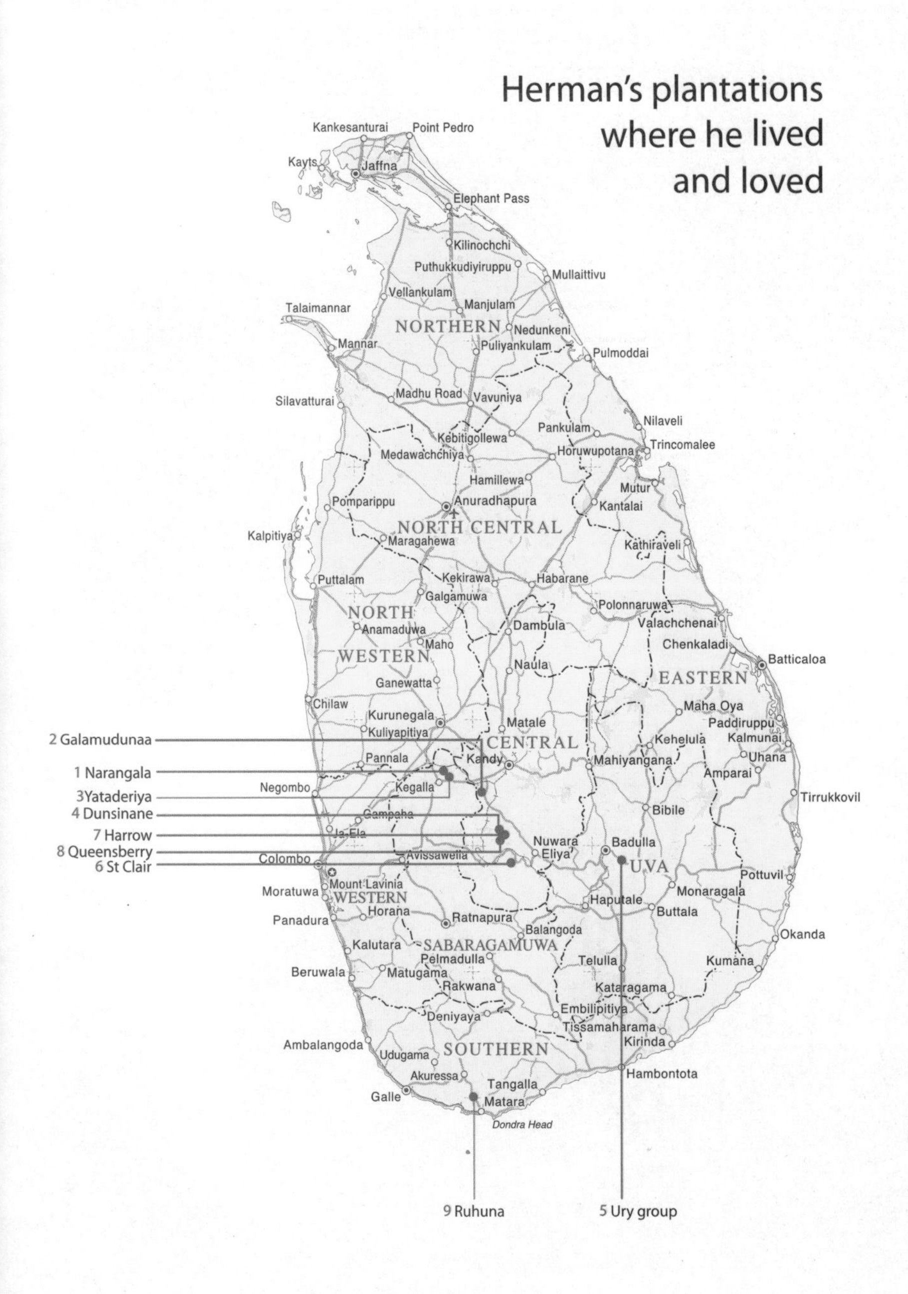
Herman's plantations
where he lived
and loved
2 Galamudunaa
1 Narangala
3Yataderiya
4 Dunsinane
7 Harrow
8 Queensberry
6 St Clair
9 Ruhuna
5 Ury group
Kankesanturai
Point Pedro
Kayts
Jaffna
Elephant Pass
Kilinochchi
Puthukkudiyiruppu
Mullaittivu
Vellankulam
Manjulam
Talaimannar
NORTHERN
Nedunkeni
Mannar
Puliyankulam
Pulmoddai
Silavatturai
Madhu Road
Vavuniya
Nilaveli
Pankulam
Kebitigollewa
Trincomalee
Medawachchiya
Horuwupotana
Hamillewa
Mutur
Pomparippu
Anuradhapura
Kantalai
Kalpitiya
NORTH CENTRAL
Maragahewa
Kathiraveli
Puttalam
Kekirawa
Habarane
Galgamuwa
Polonnaruwa
NORTH
Anamaduwa
Dambula
Valachchenai
Maho
Chenkaladi
WESTERN
Batticaloa
Naula
Ganewatta
EASTERN
Chilaw
Maha Oya
Kurunegala
Matale
Paddiruppu
Kuliyapitiya
CENTRAL
Kehelula
Kalmunai
Pannala
Kandy
Uhana
Mahiyangana
Amparai
Negombo
Kegalla
Tirrukkovil
Bibile
Gampaha
Ja-Ela
Nuwara
Eliya
Badulla
Colombo
Avissawella
UVA
Pottuvil
Mount Lavinia
Moratuwa
WESTERN
Monaragala
Haputale
Horana
Buttala
Panadura
Ratnapura
Balangoda
Okanda
Kalutara
SABARAGAMUWA
Pelmadulla
Telulla
Kumana
Beruwala
Matugama
Rakwana
Kataragama
Embilipitiya
Deniyaya
Tissamaharama
Kirinda
Ambalangoda
Udugama
SOUTHERN
Hambontota
Akuressa
Tangalla
Galle
Matara
Dondra Head

The descendants of the Suicide Club, Herman, sons and grandsons

Charitha

Migara

Maithri

Vishva

Herman

A model factory – Saint Claire, part of the fifty per cent of factories still open and possible to visit

Is this the beginning of the end? One of fifty per cent of Sri Lanka's most important foreign exchange earning factories closed and what remains has been looted

1196.000

Velaithan told him, 'Sir, that is fish called 'troot' which the English masters waste the whole day in trying to catch. They spend the entire day trying to hook a small fish of about one or two pounds. This fish you are looking at in the pond is about four pounds.'

ANA, THE TROUT FISHERMAN

The European planters made full use of Ceylon's gentle and pleasant climate. They worked hard and played hard. Every conceivable game was played on the fields of the plantation clubs. Rugby, cricket, fives and golf were all a part of the Englishman's sport.

Hunting and fishing during the weekends were eagerly looked forward to. The up-country streams were full of rainbow trout. The Trout Fishing Club in Nuwara Eliya was well stocked with fingerlings. The trout streams were well protected and only fishing club members were allowed to reel in the trout.

There were strict rules governing trout fishing, and they were carefully adhered to. If you caught a trout less than one foot in length, you had to gently remove the hook and return it to the stream. You had to make a careful note of any fish caught over one foot and report the catch to the fishing club. The club keeper, under supervision, would deposit two or three fingerlings to replenish the stock in the stream. Every trout was accounted for.

You had to use a line of about 2 lbs breaking strain so that you gave the fish a chance. It was a sport after all! You were not allowed to use live bait. It was fly fishing. There were special lures used for fishing. The most popular was the Red Admiral. The Yellow Dragonfly and the Blue Butterfly were some of the other artificial baits that I can remember if memory serves me right. I was never a trout fisherman and relate these stories through accounts by the participants and fishermen's tales told at the various clubs. Rainbow Trout made delightful eating. When a big fish was caught, photographs were taken and all the neighbours were invited to partake of the repast. If the fish was an unusually big one, it was weighed in the presence of a witness and the event recorded for the files of the fishing club. Dramatic and embellished stories were related about the long, hard battle to reel in the fish.

The trout streams flowed down from the Horton Plains to the lower areas of Lindula, Talawakelle. The streams in Bogawantalawa and Maskeliya, too, were stocked with this fighting fish. The streams were regularly patrolled by the staff of the fishing club to prevent the odd trout being caught by mischievous plantation workers. The plantation workers had a simple method of catching the trout. They hung some *tephrosia vogelli* (a leguminous plant) upstream in the water, which knocked the poor fish out unconscious. They then simply walked downstream and collected the trout floating in the water! The British planters were appalled at this home-grown technique! 'These bloody natives,' they used to utter in exasperation.

The streams and fish-rich places were given some special English names: Creek Falls, Baker's Falls, Talawakelle Rapids, Rahanwatte Rapids, Tillycoultry Cascade were some of the names that I can recall, from memory. The trout fishing rod was a long and whippy one which would make casting easy. The British planters would wear long waterproof boots so that they could wade into the water. They would don colourful clothes with a special type of cap upon which the artificial bait would be placed. A wicker basket containing the artificial bait and other angling equipment were laid by the water's edge. A small fishing card was given to every member. He had to record the date, the particular place where he was fishing, and the time he started. Feeding the stream with live bait in order to encourage the trout to a particular point was forbidden. You had to seek out the fish. The anglers adhered to all these rules with care. The rainbow trout was a good fighting game fish and a great deal of skill was necessary to reel it in. There was also a special art in casting so that you had to have the artificial bait skimming over the water to attract the fish to take the bait.

The anglers would arrive at the water's edge at the crack of dawn and fish the whole day. The trout were extremely active during the early hours of the morning and late evening. The planters had their sandwiches packed in a basket and the frugal meal was consumed by the banks of the stream in a shady spot. Every 500 yards or so, there was an angler casting upon the water. We used to pass them on the way to a friend's bungalow and wonder if these guys were crazy, wasting the whole day to catch a small fish. I have sat, however, by the Nuwara Eliya Lake, fishing for grass carp which was not so complicated, and enjoyed these tranquil moments by the water's edge. Fishing was a tonic for the tired mind.

This was an exclusive British pastime and very few Ceylonese planters indulged in the sport. Very few that is, till Ana Jayasekera took the trout fishing world by storm!

Ana, the expert fine diner, was a very successful planter. From Mocha Estate, Maskeliya, he climbed rapidly in the company to become the Manager of Loinorn Estate, Bogowantalawa. Loinorn was a very special plantation, situated in Ceylon's Golden Valley. Bogawantalawa, which was famous for the production of top quality teas.

Myriad trout streams criss-crossed the valley, and cascaded down to the Mahaweli, Ceylon's 'river of life.' Ana was right in the middle of trout country and he had heard many trout stories at the Bogawantalawa Planters' Club. He had never stepped into a trout stream in his life although he was to catch the biggest fish recorded in the history of the fishing club.

The trout can only thrive in flowing water. While walking round the Loinorn garden and relaxing near a largish pond, Ana had noticed a huge fish breaking the water. He quickly summoned his gardener, Velaithan, and told him that he had seen a big fish in the pond. The pond had a sluice where the water used to flow in and flow out back into a stream. Velaithan told him, "Sir, that is fish called 'troot' which the English masters waste the whole day in trying to catch. They waste the whole day and catch a small fish of about one or two pounds. This fish in the pond is about four pounds." This was grist to Ana's mill. There was a wooden plug at the bottom of the pond which was occasionally removed to clean it out. Ana then spat on his hands, rolled up his sleeves and set to work. The British anglers fished alone. Ana was going to have an assistant angler: his gardener, Velaithan.

"Velaithan," he ordered. "Get a stout *dadap* stick about four feet long, and pull out the plug holding the water in the pond."

By now, Velaithan realised what the master was going to do. "Why master?" he queried aghast, as he guessed what Ana's intentions were.

"You do as you are told," Ana ordered.

With great difficulty Velaithan removed the plug and the water started gushing out. After about an hour the pond was almost empty and there was the trout thrashing about in the mud. Ana clobbered the trout with the *dadap* stick and in a moment he triumphantly retrieved the lifeless fish from the pond.

This was sacrilege in the eyes of Velaithan, since he knew with what care Anas predecessor had fed and looked after the trout. The fish was affectionately called Peter. Ana clouted Peter.

He had bigger plans for the

Traditional tea basket's keep the green leaves aerated

fish. He obtained the services of a well-trained cook from the plantations and slow fried the trout in wine sauce and dressed it up with salad leaves and mint sauce. Having made a record catch, Ana was not going to eat the trout by himself. He was going to tell the world the story of his awesome feat.

Mrs. Gordon was the wife of a wealthy retired planter. She decided to remain in Ceylon after her husband's demise. She inherited her husband's fortune and was popularly known as the Duchess. The planters addressed her as Ma Gordon. Her home was a refuge for the young planters. She was, however, very choosy about her house guests. Ma Gordon was very fond of Ana, the mischievous Sinhalese planter. Ana had pride of place in the Gordon home. Ma Gordon used to laugh her sides out at Ana's tales. No party of Ma Gordon's was ever complete without Ana on the guest list. When she had guests she used to prevail upon Ana to relate tales of his experiences with the Mossops. She had an impish sense of humour and was able to laugh uproariously at the foibles of her countrymen in Ceylon. An invitation to the Gordon home for a party was highly coveted and the planters used to wonder how Ana made it on every occasion. Ana made it because he had no pretensions and was able not only to laugh at himself but also at others without a tinge of malice. It was simply good fun.

Ana placed Peter on an elegant silver tray, waltzed triumphantly to Ma Gordon's bungalow and presented the fish to the Duchess. "Oh, Ananda, what a wonderful gift. I have never seen such a big trout caught in our waters. I did not know that you were such a good angler. Where did you catch the fish and what fly did you use?" Ma Gordon excitedly asked Ana. She was more than surprised at the size of the fish. She never realised that the home-grown Ana could wield a trout fishing rod so cleverly.

This was where Ana spun his tale. "There was an old rod and some tackle left behind by my predecessor on Loinorn. I was practising casting on my lawn. When I thought I had mastered the art I ventured out to the Bogawantalawa stream that runs by the side of Loinorn. I have been trying my luck for some time and I have caught many small fish but I was waiting for the big one. On the third occasion I felt as if lightning had struck the rod. The fish took most of the line away and I had to fight it gradually for almost half an hour before I could reel it in. I used a Red Admiral and a two pound breaking strain line," went on Ana the Angler. Ana was piling up on his story. Ma Gordon was looking at Ana in utter, undiluted admiration.

"You wait till I meet Geoff Middleton and Peter Easteal and tell them of your exploits. They spend almost a day in the water and most times come back with nothing. Never a whopper like this. At most, the biggest fish I have seen was a two pounder caught by Dick Hazell. It takes real skill to catch a fish like this. Did you take a photograph of you coming out of the water with the fish?" asked Mrs. Gordon.

"No, Ma, I did not do that."

"You should have, Ana," she remarked.

A photograph of the event would have landed him in trouble. In the first place, he was not a member of the Fishing Club. He was simply a poacher. Ana wielding a *dadap* stick and clobbering the trout would have been sacrilegious in the eyes of the real trout fisherman. 'Not done old chap,' they would have intoned, and looked down their noses with disdain at this fish killer!

Ana took in all this praise and admiration, looking like the cat that swallowed the canary!

This tale should have ended there. But it did not. He went to the Bogawantalawa Club the next week and bragged to the Ceylonese planters about how he clobbered the trout with a stick and later presented it to Ma Gordon. "The old lady asked me what fly I used and I told her it was a Red Admiral. What bloody Red Admiral for me, this is the first time that I saw a trout in my life! She told me to write to the wildlife journal about how I caught this fish. I dared not do that because if you b_____s had seen the article you would have known that I was spinning a tale."

Peter Easteal and Geoff Middleton had visited Ma Gordon after an abortive day's fishing and were talking to her about 'the one that got away.' It was then that Ma Gordon told them about Ana's exploits. "You know young Ana Jayasekera on Loinorn? He has taken to trout fishing lately, and had caught the most whopping big four pounder only the other day. He used a Red Admiral and he was fishing at the Bogo stream. A fine young chap, this Jayasekera. He not only caught this fish but presented it to me cooked in red wine sauce." She extolled the virtues of Ana's ability as an angler.

Geoff and Peter visited the Bogo Club that evening and after a couple of drinks asked the members if Ana Jayasekera was around. They spoke his name almost in awe. Ana was not at the club that day. Sumeda Jayasinghe (not his real name) of Campion asked the two British planters why they were looking for Ana. "Oh, Ma Gordon says he is one of the best anglers in the area and we want to meet him." They went on to tell them about Ana's four pounder, Red Admiral and all.

Sumeda had heard from Ana himself about the clobbering he gave the trout with a *dadap* stick. "What bloody Red Admiral does Ana know about? He whacked the poor fish in the Loinorn pond and later presented it to the old lady, making up this tall story."

I cannot recall if the two British planters related the true story to Ma Gordon. When Ana heard about Sumeda's betrayal he did not abuse him but had some pithy things to say about his parents!

One never betrays one's own. I am sure Sumeda Jayasinghe, too, saw the humour in the incident and did not intend this betrayal maliciously.

Ana's trout fishing days were over. He never waded into the water again.

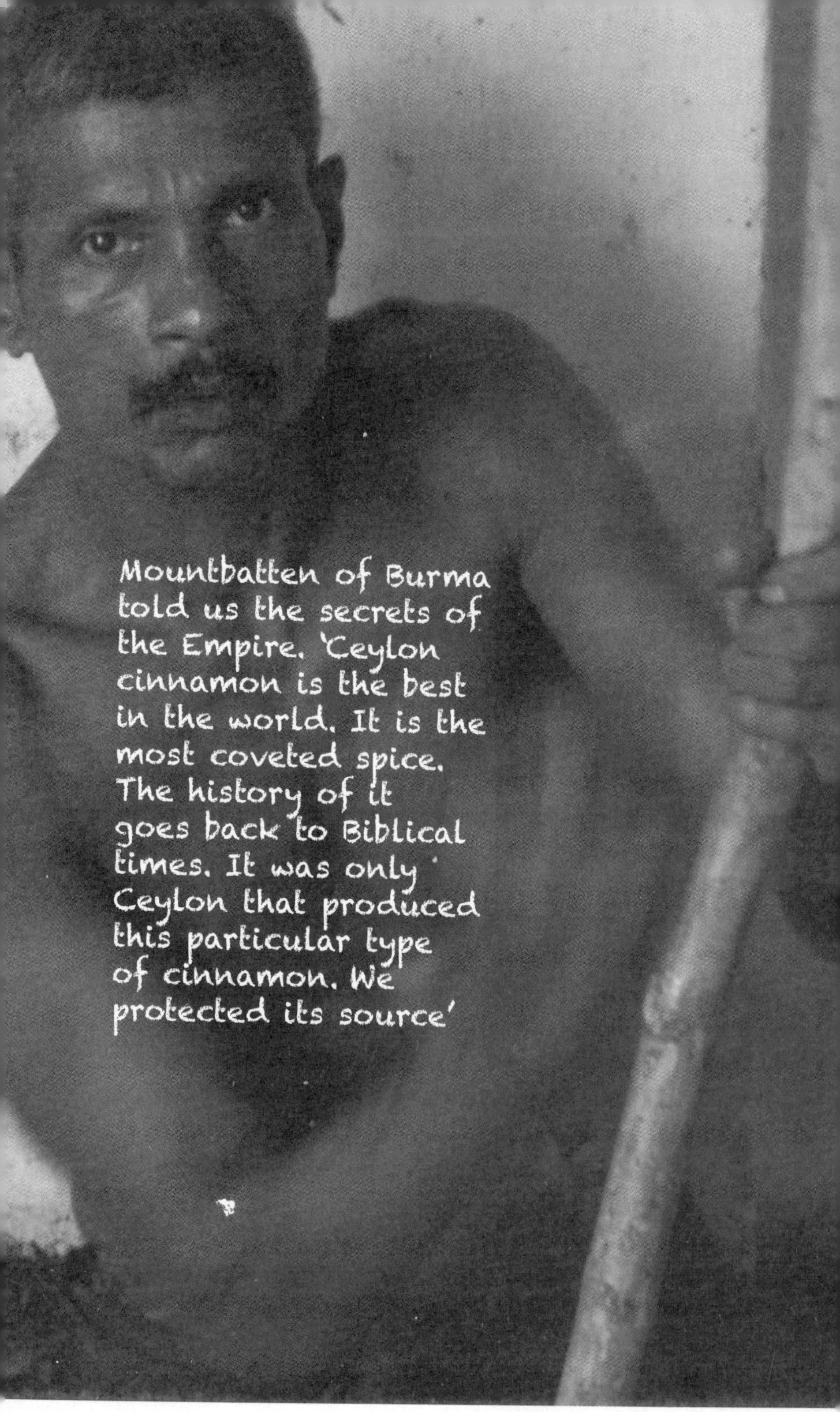

Mountbatten of Burma told us the secrets of the Empire. 'Ceylon cinnamon is the best in the world. It is the most coveted spice. The history of it goes back to Biblical times. It was only Ceylon that produced this particular type of cinnamon. We protected its source'

MOUNTBATTEN OF BURMA - ADMIRAL OF THE FLEET

From Ury Group, Passara, I was transferred on promotion to St. Clair Estate, Talawakelle, and from St. Clair to Harrow Estate, Punduloya. After a couple of years I was again transferred to Queensberry Estate, Kotmale. All of these promotions were to bigger and better properties. Most of my planting life was spent in the Kotmale Valley.

Kotmale is a mist-laden meadow. Ceylon's eternal hero, King Dutugemunu, also called Abhaya Gamini sought refuge in Kotmale when he had a disagreement with his father, King Kavantissa. Kotmale will always be home to me. It was King Dutugemunu who brought Ceylon under one flag by defeating King Elara of Jaffna. I sometimes felt that in a journey through *Samsara* (previous birth), I had marched with Dutugemunu's army to free the country from a divided rule. There is a true story about our struggle to free Ceylon from being divided in a book that I wrote, entitled, *For A Sovereign State*. I have recounted this story. When the Ceylon police were looking high and low for me I, too, sought refuge in Kotmale. It was one of the most fertile places in Ceylon. I am truly a son of Kotmale. Even now, at the first available opportunity, I flee to Kotmale. Dutugemunu, like me, was a son of Ruhuna, who ultimately found solace in this mist-laden valley. President J. R. Jayewardene of modern Sri Lanka referred to me when a document of mine was given to him by my friend, Sinha Ratnatunga, and said, 'Oh, so this is from Dutugemunu.' It was the story of our fight for a Sovereign State. Permit me, reader, this digression. Kotmale has this effect on me.

It was to Kotmale that another King returned. This was Lord Louis Mountbatten of Burma, Viceroy of India and Ceylon, Supreme Allied Commander, the chosen representative of King George, Emperor of the British Empire. He was born Louis Francis Albert Victor Nicholas Mountbatten and was the first Sea Lord of the British Empire. His father was Prince Louis Battenberg and his mother was Princess Victoria of Hesse. His

grandparents were Prince Alexander of Hesse and Princess Julia of Battenberg. He was very conscious of his royal lineage and one of his main foibles was the accumulation of titles! That is the reason I have listed his titles and lineage in full.

Dimbula Estate, Patana, was next to Queensberry. The Manager, Mervyn Jayasinghe, was my friend. The Governor General's office suddenly telephoned Mervyn and informed him that Lord Louis Mountbatten would like to pay a visit to Dimbula Estate and requested Mervyn to provide lunch for the Supreme Commander and his party. Mervyn was taken by surprise but readily agreed. It later transpired that Dimbula Estate was the Viceroy's hill station resort during the Second World War. He was coming back to visit his old secret hideout. None of us knew that Lord Mountbatten had lived at the Dimbula bungalow.

Mervyn invited me to join the lunch party. To Barney, Mervyn's wife, this was no big deal. She was an accomplished host and providing lunch for the Admiral of the Fleet was as easy as falling off a log. She took it in her stride.

We had a problem, Mervyn and I. What were we going to wear for the occasion? Casual clothes, shirt and tie or a full lounge suit? I was going for casual clothes. It was a beautiful balmy morning with the sun shining brightly. However, Mervyn, more on the side of caution, told me that the two of us should be in full lounge suit as a mark of respect to the King Emperor. Mervyn was my teacher and my steadfast friend in many matters. I readily agreed. Mervyn also instructed me to come to his bungalow as early as possible to greet the visiting Supreme Commander.

The day of the Supreme Commander's visit dawned. Barney had decided that the morning drinks would be served on the sprawling manicured lawn of Dimbula. A dressed up table was laid out to hold a variety of drinks that Mervyn had chosen. Champagne, vintage wines, choice whiskies, cut glass decanters and elegant ice bowls all came out of Mervyn's cellar. Barney was laying it on good and thick. "Why all this cut glass for Mountbatten when we have to drink in glass tumblers and take the ice off plastic bowls?" I joked with Mervyn and Barney. Barney replied, also in jest, "I dare not bring out the cut glass for you. You may drop the bloody glasses, and you would not even know how to use them."

The expected time of arrival was 10.30am. Right on the dot, the Supreme Commander's *entourage* entered the Dimbula bungalow. They were travelling from the King's Pavilion in Kandy. The party consisted of five people. Lord Louis Mountbatten, his daughter Lady Patricia Brabourne, her husband Lord Brabourne, and another lady, who I think was a friend. They were accompanied by the Naval Commander William Molegoda, ADC to the Governor General and now ADC in attendance to the Supreme Commander. Commander Molegoda was in full ceremonial naval attire.

Lord Louis wore a smart, cotton short sleeved shirt and cotton slacks. He was also wearing a pair of very expensive but comfortable leather shoes. Lady Patricia and her husband, Lord Brabourne, were also dressed quite elegantly but with absolute simplicity.

Mervyn and I were boiling in the noon day sun in our dark lounge suits, feeling completely inferior. Overdressing was worse than under-dressing. I slowly whispered to him that we may look like two funeral undertakers and asked whether we could both quietly get rid of the jackets. We gradually shed our jackets and ties and began to feel far more comfortable. A bottle of vintage Champagne was placed in a cut glass bucket of ice with silver ice tongs to match. Mervyn asked Lord Louis what he would like to drink and suggested a bottle of Champagne. "I would really like a glass of beer," said the Royal Knight. Mervyn had a variety of beers and he was just about to open a bottle of Carlsberg beer. "Do you have any Nuwara Eliya beer?" enquired Lord Louis. Mervyn served him his preferred drink. The others went for gin and tonics.

The Supreme Allied Commander thus set the tone for the morning. He was thoroughly relaxed and seemed to be at home in his old secret hideout. He went on to tell us about his stay in Ceylon. What impressed me most about this remarkable man was his simplicity. Six foot in height and handsome, with a towering personality, he was soft spoken and charming. Never overbearing, it was a lesson to the Ceylon politician about demeanour and deportment. He put Mervyn completely at ease. "Mervyn," he said, "it is a real pleasure for me to return to the Dimbula bungalow. It is just as I left it almost 40 years ago. I must compliment you for maintaining such excellent high standards. You know Dimbula was my secret hideout and I used to come here alone, with my family and sometimes with one or two of my important general staff to map out our campaigns in the Far East and to review the progress of the war. Dimbula was kept a secret even from the British Army, and when I was Supreme Allied Commander of the British Expeditionary forces, my headquarters were in Kandy at the Peradeniya Gardens."

Lord Louis was specially selected for the task of resolving the conflict between India, a predominantly Hindu country, and Pakistan, which was a Muslim state. His appointment had the imprimatur of King George, his cousin, but was eventually made by the Prime Minister, Clement Atlee. The Minister of War was Sir Winston Churchill. In typical British fashion, Clement Atlee did not want to offend Churchill and afterwards it was decided to send Lord Louis to India as Viceroy. They wanted Churchill to offer him the appointment once again. Churchill and Mountbatten both had enormous egos and were strong personalities. Lord Louis was certainly not a fan of Churchill. One day Sir Winston summoned him to the War Office and told him that the King Emperor wanted him appointed as Viceroy of India.

'Will you accept it?' he enquired, lording it over Mountbatten.

'I will need two weeks to make a decision,' replied the Supreme Commander, playing out the charade.

'Why, do you think you are not up to the job?' Churchill queried sarcastically.

Mountbatten retorted with a sharp dart thrown on target at Churchill. 'Unfortunately I have a congenital weakness that makes me believe that I can do anything, but I still need my two weeks.'

With one fell swoop he put Churchill in his place.

Muhammed Ali Jinnah was the leader of Pakistan and Jawaharlal Nehru was the leader of India. Both countries were part of the mighty British Empire. India and Pakistan were ruled as one country but it was becoming increasingly evident that they wanted to go their separate ways. It was the intention of Her Majesty's government that a political settlement had to be reached to resolve this simmering conflict. Sir Winston Churchill was the Minister of War. He was against the partition of India and he appeared to be partial to Muslim Pakistan.

The magic of the moment was not lost on me. I was a student of history of the British Empire. Here were a few of us having a gin and tonic with one of the greatest men of history. I am seldom impressed by politicians. They symbolise power, that awful human trait which makes men creep and crawl. Lord Louis Mountbatten had all the trappings of power. He came from a distinguished royal lineage. He was the cousin of the King. He was an extremely handsome soldier. But he also had great humility, as I was to learn later.

During the course of the discussions he told us how pleasant Ceylon was. "I loved the hospitality of your country. We considered Ceylon to be the most prized possession of the British crown, so much so that we did not make it known that this was a part of the Empire. We liked to call it a part of India. As a naval man I realised the strategic importance of your country, particularly Trincomalee. It is the best natural harbour in the world. You can take in the biggest ships to

Trincomalee and once they enter the large natural coves, they are completely camouflaged from aerial reconnaissance. He who controls Trincomalee holds sway over the whole South East Asian region," said the Admiral of the Fleet.

He told us the secrets of the Empire. "Ceylon cinnamon is the best in the world. It is the most coveted spice. The history of it goes back to Biblical times. It was only Ceylon that produced this particular type of cinnamon. We protected its source so jealously that we sent the cinnamon stocks by boat to Madras and shipped it out to the world from there to conceal the true source."

He went on, "Some of the most precious blue sapphires, which are a part of the Royal collection came from Ratnapura." This man had a remarkable memory. He remembered place names and people very vividly after so many years.

We were all to receive the most pleasant and most touching example of this memory. He asked Mervyn permission to walk into the Dimbula sitting room. "I remember the place where my secret radio communication set was concealed," he said, and walked to a particular spot in the morning room. With Mervyn's approval he yanked out a plank on the boarded floor and there was a hollow space of about three square feet which held the secret radio set. We were looking at this man in undisguised awe.

That was not all. "Mervyn," he said, "you have been so kind to me. Can I ask you a favour? I had an old gardener who was also my close aide. He was from the Upper Division. His name was Sinniah, and he would be about my age. Can you please try to locate him for me? I would really like to see him." Here was Lord Louis Mountbatten, First Sea Lord, Admiral of the Fleet, Supreme Allied Commander, Viceroy of India, asking us to find his humble gardener for him.

This was a tall order, but we could not do enough for this gentle man. The name Sinniah, on a plantation, was like a

It's like tasting wine

Smith or Jones in England. There must have been at least three dozen Sinniahs on the Upper Division. Mervyn deployed me to trace Sinniah. After an age comparison and a process of elimination I located the two likely candidates. Then I enquired from them if they had ever worked for Mountbatten *Dorai* (Master). One guy, whom I had shanghaied from a cattle shed, said to me, 'Sir, you are referring to the *Raja* (King). I was his *tottakaran* (gardener). He was like a god,' declared Sinniah.

I told him that the Commander was in the big bungalow and that he wanted to meet him.

Sinniah who was not the picture of sartorial elegance, having just emerged from the cattle shed, wanted to change his clothes before accompanying me to the big bungalow. I did not want to miss even a moment with the Supreme Commander and told Sinniah, "No, it does not matter. He wants you to come as you are, as soon as possible."

I bundled Sinniah into Mervyn's car and took him down to the Dimbula Bungalow. I gave the thumbs up signal triumphantly to Mervyn, confirming that I had found Sinniah.

Sinniah got out of the car. Lord Louis walked from the party to greet his friend.

"Raja vantha irikaran," (the King has come) cried Sinniah, with hands held aloft in veneration and worship, and he fell at Mountbatten's feet. The Supreme Commander embraced the humble Sinniah with great affection.

Can you try to imagine the magic of this moment? Lord Louis, who had ruled almost a billion people in India, Ceylon and Burma, then comes over to Dimbula 40 years later and remembers his old gardener and wants to see him. We were so touched witnessing this very moving scene. This is the most important lesson in humility and simplicity that I have learnt in my whole life. Compare this with the ego-bloated, strutting politicians of our day and then you will know what makes the difference between obscurity and greatness - between mere politicians and statesmen, and between mice and men.

That was not all. Lord Mountbatten of Burma, Admiral of the Fleet, the Viceroy of India and Ceylon posed for a photograph with Sinniah of the Upper Division of Dimbula Estate. Commander William Molegoda, the ADC in attendance, was requested to take the photograph. "William," the gentle night told his ADC, "Please develop this photograph. I would like to sign it and give it to Sinniah." And that was how one of the most memorable events in my life - the meeting with Lord Mountbatten, ended.

We all sat down to lunch exhilarated by the occasion and a little tipsy after a few drinks, and partook of Barney's wonderful rice and curry over which Lord Louis expressed lavish praise and appreciation.

After lunch and coffee, the visitors were getting ready to leave Dimbula. Mervyn went up to the party and proffered the Visitors' Book to the Knight Royal. The date was the 14th of February 1976. This was what he wrote in the Visitors' Book:

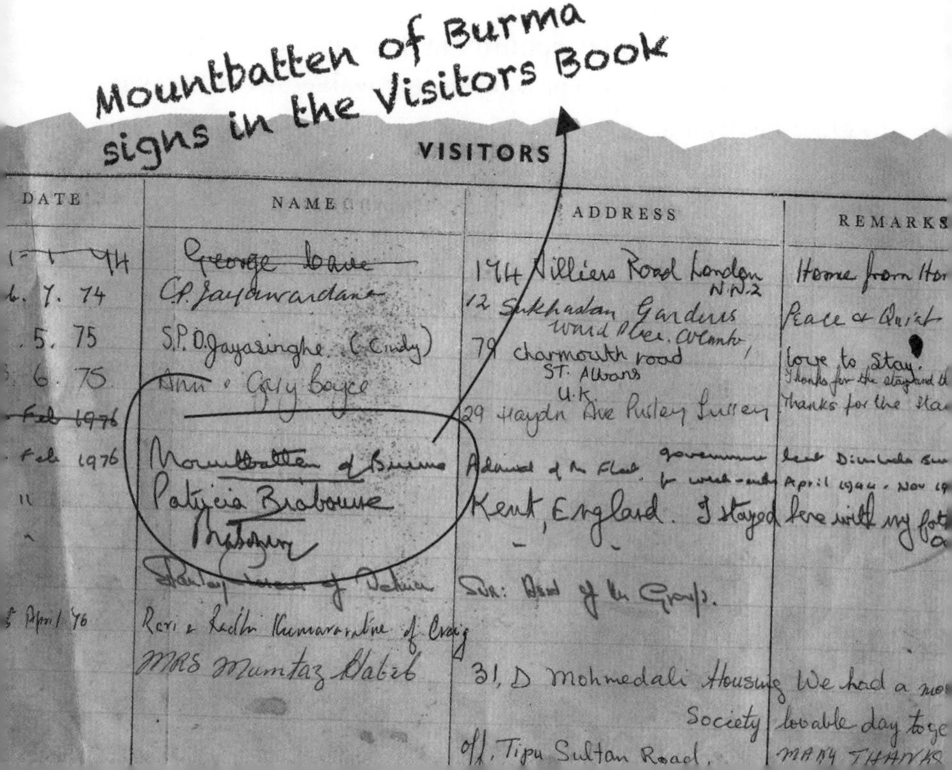

Mountbatten of Burma signs in the Visitors Book

Admiral of the Fleet
The government lent the Dimbula Bungalow for weekends,
April 1944 to November 1945

Lady Patricia wrote:

Patricia Brabourne
Kent, England

I stayed here with my father in October 1945

There was a very interesting sequel to this entry and the Supreme Commander's visit. The next visitor to the Dimbula Bungalow was my very old planting friend, Stanley Perera. He was also a friend of Mervyn's, having been Mervyn's assistant on Delmar Estate, Uda Pusellawa. Stanley could not understand why we were still talking about Lord Louis' visit. He was somewhat deficient in the history department. "Who the hell is this Mountbatten?" he irreverently asked us and, not to be outdone, wrote in the visitors' book:

Stanley Perera of Delmar, Snr. Assistant of the Group, copied the way Mountbatten wrote his title. We used to dine out on this story for many years to come, and do so even today!

On the final occasion
when he fell, he glanced
up at his son who, with
tears in his eyes at the
beating that the father
was receiving, was still
cheering, 'Get up Daddy.'
The film was The Champ

I CHANGED COURSE

The tea *kadé* – the gossip centre in the village

'Two prisoners look out through the same bars, one sees the mud, one sees the stars'

This is only about the stars. My life as a planter and my rise in the profession was a great deal more harrowing and difficult than has been made out in this book. However, I was very much a product of the Raj, and leaving out my participation in some events where I was a ringside player, would detract from the story. This chapter is not so much to talk about my achievements but about the fast moving political landscape and how it affected the plantations. If there are some disproportionate references to myself, I crave the reader's indulgence. I make those references just in order to tell the story.

The plantations were nationalised in 1976, but the agency houses continued to manage the estates for the state. This was for a very short period, before the two state agencies were born: the Sri Lanka State Plantations Corporation (SLSPC) and the Janatha Estates Development Board (JEDB).

It was during the last days of agency house management that I was appointed, at 29 years of age, the youngest Manager of

Dunsinane Estate. This was an appointment on merit, as were all my previous appointments. I worked my heart out on this property and produced some outstanding results. No achievement in the management of a large estate could be attributed to the ability of one man. I had some very able and dedicated assistants. Ravi Kotelawala, Aubrey Patternott and Tyronne Perera are some of the names I can recall. Special mention must also be made of Dr. A. Ramanathan, the Resident Medical Officer on Dunsinane. He was my eyes and ears on the property and I wanted him to keep me and the assistants informed of the slightest tremors. Dr. Ramanathan did this sometimes with frank brutality, but always in the best interests of the property. Last but not least, it is to the labour force that the real tribute has to be paid. They worked long hours to obtain the highest ever recorded crops on the estate. There was not a single day of labour unrest. In fact, when the trade unions called for sympathy strikes concerning general matters, the workers asked me for my permission to go on strike! I did not attempt to dissuade them.

It was on Dunsinane that Hugette came into my life and stabilised a rather reckless lifestyle of late nights and heavy drinking at the various clubs. My personal life began to assume some order and purpose with Hugette's gentle presence. She was extremely fond of my two sons, Maithri and Vishva (Uchi being his pet name).

She showered me with the most expensive gifts. Hand made shirts from Jean Fabrice and Yves St. Laurent. Perfumes like Eau Savage from Christian Dior, and Givenchy, suits from the best fashion houses on the Champs-Élysées. The irony was not lost on me: I had gone from the ill-attired Creeper on Narangalla to possibly the most elegantly-dressed planter in the hills. Strange are the ways of fortune and destiny, I thought.

She gifted only the best and the most expensive clothes, not found anywhere in Ceylon. I had to get dressed and stand before her before going out in the evening. 'Oui, you are smart and handsome, you ugly man,' she would say, giving me her approval.

She, however, never joined me to meet any of my friends or to go for any ceremonial occasions. 'I come three times a year to Ceylon not to see your friends and go to clubs but to be with you, Maithri and Uchi. Come back early without getting too drunk,' she would gently warn me. This added to the mystery. My friends had only seen her flashing past in my car, very strikingly beautiful, but never met her. The most fascinating thing about Hugette was the French accent. There is nothing so enchanting as a French woman speaking English!

She took Uchi for holidays in France and taught him French. On one occasion, she took him to Grenoble to show him the snow, which he had not seen. They were staying in an elegant hotel and when they sat down to dinner she had the brilliant idea of getting him, a small boy of about 12 years, to make a speech in French to all those gathered for dinner.

Uchi, in his halting French, made the speech. 'I am Uchi from Ceylon. I am in your country with my Poupy. This is the first time I have seen snow. I like France and the people. They have been very kind to me. Bon appetite.' His very short speech met with loud applause from all those present. He was to make many speeches and addresses to the judges and juries of the law courts in Ceylon. I am sure he will remember the one in Grenoble as the most memorable. I asked Hugette what made her do this. 'I wanted him to know that a good-looking boy who has confidence will be accepted anywhere in the world. I also wanted to help him build up confidence in himself.' That she did.

I had made no provision for the future, nor thought about life after the plantations or how we were going to survive if I were to leave the plantations abruptly. She, in her own way, realised that I may just do this, without rhyme or reason, in a sudden fit of provocation. This concern for my future began, strangely, after a film that the four of us went to see.

The film was *The Champ*. It was the story of a single father. A boxer who had one son of whom he was passionately fond. He was having a run of bad luck, losing fight after fight and nobody

In those days phoning was like sending smoke signals. The connections overlapped and eaves dropping was rampant with naughty planters' wives revealing some pretty sordid secrets

wanted to sponsor him any more. He had only one fan. That was his son.

The boxer, 'the champ,' agreed to take on a famous opponent at a fight where the prize money was high. He was determined to win the prize money to stash it away as a fund for educating the love of his life, his only son. He was out of training and had not won a fight for a long time. All the odds were against him.

The fight started with the boxer getting the beating of his life from his opponent. The only guy cheering him was his son, standing by the ring. 'Come on Daddy, you can do it. Don't give up, you are the best boxer in the world. I know you can do it.' The boxer was felled to the ground on more than two occasions and he was completely bloodied up, lips swollen and mouth cracked, and gasping for breath. On the final occasion when he fell, he glanced up at his son who, with tears in his eyes at the beating that the father was receiving, was still cheering, 'Get up Daddy. You can do it. I know you can do it!'

The boxer got up one last time from the canvas. He went for his opponent with everything he had and, with one last spurt of sustained fighting, knocked him out of contention. He looked at his little son after the fight and gasped, 'That one was for you.' Hugette was strangely silent after this moving film. At dinner that night she told my sons, 'You know who the boxer reminds me of? Your father. He will risk everything he has on one last fight. He has won all his fights up to now but he may one day lose the last fight of his life. We must all think about his future, since he is not going to do it.' It was after seeing *The Champ* that I bought my first coconut property in Nattandiya as a provision for the future.

There were many others who assisted me, but the gentle Hugette was the one, the only one, who made the difference.

I had made many mistakes in the past. On Dunsinane I left all this behind me and started afresh. My first guiding principle was absolute justice to all. A large plantation is like a Kingdom. Three thousand people depend on you for their livelihood. You hold the power to change their lives for better or worse. 'Do unto

others as you would have others do unto you' was my guiding philosophy. All previous enmities, prejudices and dislikes were forgotten. After all, this same labour force demanded my removal from Dunsinane! I set out to be fair even to those who fought me bitterly. This paid enormous dividends and after some time I had the labour force doing exactly as I wanted. In fact, my friend Radha Mathavan had one day asked a Jaffna school teacher on Dunsinane how I was faring. His reply was, '*Yejaman nithiya are sangatha konduporara*' (The King is ruling the government with absolute justice). When Radha told me this episode I was happier than receiving the best accolade from the Chairman, Sir John Arbuthnot.

The general election was held in the year 1977. I was always a supporter of the left wing Sri Lanka Freedom Party. However, I saw the naked nepotism and mismanagement of the government of the day and was disillusioned with the party that I supported.

At that time my neighbouring estate was Sheen Group, Punduloya. The Manager appointed to that property was Pem Seneviratne. He was a very close friend of the Prime Ministerial candidate J. R. Jayewardene, who won the election and later went on to become Ceylon's first President. When J. R. Jayewardene visited Sheen Group I was regularly invited to dinner. Pem used to get me to imitate my friend Thondaman to J. R. Jayewardene and everybody would roll in laughter. I was introduced to JRJ as a strong supporter of the opposing political party, who was disillusioned with them. "Why don't you support the United National Party?" Mr. Jayewardene asked me. I had one problem in doing this. The Member of Parliament for Kotmale was J. D. Weerasekera. He was my very good friend and I found it difficult to oppose him. JD was also not happy with the way his party was going and had told me that he was not contesting that election. "If JD is not contesting, I will very definitely support you," I said.

JRJ was a cultured man, a man of great learning, and had a tremendous personality. He was very quietly confident that he would soon be Prime Minister. He was a man who had spent

his entire life in Ceylon politics and was the last freedom fighter alive. It was he and a few others who were in the forefront of the freedom struggle to obtain independence for Ceylon from the British Empire. JD did not contest and I plunged into the deep end of the murky waters of politics. Having been in Kotmale for over 25 years I had some influence in the area.

JRJ was a meticulous planner. He left nothing to chance. He wanted Pem to introduce me to Gamini Dissanayaka, a rising political star who was spearheading the campaign in Nuwara Eliya-Maskeliya, the largest electorate in the country.

Opposing Gamini was Anura Bandaranaike, Prime Minister Sirimavo Bandaranaike's son. His father and mother were both Prime Ministers of independent Ceylon. His sister later went onto to become Ceylon's first woman President. The tide was slowly turning against the ruling party and Gamini was leading the charge in the up-country.

The two state plantation management organisations that came into being were very highly politicised. All appointments were based on political or family loyalties to the Bandaranaike family and the Sri Lanka Freedom Party. We were watching these developments with grave concern. It was absolutely clear that the days of meritocracy were over. There was a creeping sense of uncertainty.

Gamini was taking the fight to the government and they were getting desperate to retain power. The Nuwara Eliya-Maskeliya electorate was comprised of a majority of Indian Tamil plantation workers. It was becoming quite evident that this community, led by Thondaman, was throwing its full weight behind J. R. Jayewardene. Thondaman was the shrewdest tactician in the business and he had an iron grip on the plantation community.

His father, Karuppiah, was the Head Kangany on Wavendon Estate, Ramboda. It was men like Karuppiah who made the long march from India to Ceylon, bringing labour on foot from Mannar to the Ceylon Highlands and marching through elephant country. Many fell on the wayside due to exhaustion. Others succumbed

to malaria. The Head Kangany was the supplier of labour to the plantations, and he had immense power. It was then that the government of the day came up with the idea of alienating 10,000 acres of the island's best tea lands to the Sinhalese villagers.

We, who had lived on the plantations most of our lives, realised the inherent dangers in this suicidal attempt. The land alienation was to be done before the elections, and was an obvious attempt to win the favour of the Sinhalese voters. A list was prepared by the political authority in the district, apportioning the acreage to be alienated from each estate. This was a confidential document but was leaked to me by a powerful friend in the government. The government was trying to soften the blow by saying that it was only the uncultivated and infertile land that was earmarked for distribution. The document in my possession gave the lie to that story.

We realised that the even tenor on the plantations would be completely destroyed by this arbitrary act. To give plantation land exclusively to the Sinhalese would fuel racial tensions which would have catastrophic consequences.

A few of us met at the Holyrood Estate bungalow to discuss what action we should take. The Manager of Holyrood was Rohan Wijeyanayaka. My good friend and school mate, P.H.A.N. Dias, was the Ceylon Planters' Society (CPS) head of the area. This was a secret meeting as there were those on the plantations who were supportive of this government's scheme of land distribution, and we ran the real risk of victimisation if our intentions were revealed at these initial stages. This meeting later came to be known as the 'Holyrood Conference.'

All those invited attended the conference including Pem Seneviratne, Rohan Wijeyanaike, Aubrey Tissera, Ralston Tissera and M. H. K. Jagathsena. Altogether there were about 15 senior planters from the Nuwara Eliya-Maskeliya district. They represented every sub-district in the region. We decided to obtain their views on the proposed land take-over. There was anger and disbelief at what the government was trying to do.

Some planters told us how Sinhalese villagers were already visiting the estates surreptitiously and identifying the lands that they would eventually select. We were not going to suggest any course of action without the idea first coming from those present. I realised that we would be taking on the government headlong in this effort and wanted to be sure that there was unity among us. After a long and protracted discussion, it was agreed to resist the land take-over comprehensively with whatever strength we had. However, it was decided to obtain the views of all the planters in the district before we proceeded further. Everyone was extremely concerned about the tension that existed between the Tamil plantation workers and the Sinhalese villagers due to this indiscriminate land alienation. The Tamil workers who were the majority, always considered the plantation on which they worked to be their heritage. Hordes of villagers walking into the plantations would most definitely have been resisted. The conflict that ensued would set off violence throughout the entire plantation areas.

Over and above all of all this, the workers informed us that if this land take-over went ahead, they themselves would be staking a claim for the land. We had anticipated this. We first decided to make known these fears to the Government Agent of Nuwara Eliya. If that did not have the desired result, we resolved to summon a meeting of the entire plantation community to the Nuwara Eliya Golf Club. A skeletal plan of a protest march to Colombo was discussed. I was also told to contact my friend, Thondaman, to put in some muscle to these protests. I agreed to do this and met him at his Wavendon bungalow. "The government is desperate. They want to go ahead with the land take-over at any cost," I told him.

"Talking to the Government Agent is good for the record but nothing is going to happen," Thondaman stated. "I will support you in this with the might of the workforce in the plantations, but we have to work out a strategy that achieves the objective. You will have to stall this till after the elections are over and then

a new government will come in and the issue will die a natural death." Ever the pragmatist, Thondaman recommended a stalling operation.

I told him that the entire plantation community in Ceylon was planning a protest march to Colombo to meet the Prime Minister. "That is a good idea but she will not meet you, and neither will the Minister of Plantation Industries. You must get the maximum media exposure to the possible consequences of this act. I will also support you on that. You must then ask to meet the Inspector General of Police. It is the Inspector General who will be responsible to the new government for law and order. He knows the way the wind is blowing. Put the responsibility entirely on him. Don't waste your time with the politicians. They are on a 'do or die' mission. Make it very clear to the IGP that he will have to advise the government that the violence and unrest in the hills will escalate if they go on with this scheme," he recommended. I then told him about the proposed meeting at the Golf Club and requested him to be present. Thondaman agreed to come.

The day of the Golf Club meeting dawned. Planters from the four corners of the island were present. Aelian De Silva, my former boss and the chairman of the Ceylon Planters' Society (the trade union of the planters) was chairing the meeting and wanted to obtain the sentiments of those present without in any way persuading them to take a course of action which they might regret later on. He explained the situation in the Nuwara Eliya district as the proposed land alienation was to take place initially in Nuwara Eliya. The meetings at the Golf Club were quite lively because the participants had easy recourse to the well-stocked bar.

There were no restrictions in the liquor department and by the time the meeting started, the plantation managers were 'nine sheets to the wind.' There was a chorus of support for the protest march to Colombo. 'This must be resisted at any cost,' was the mandate given. The more sober ones enquired if we could also get the plantation workers to join in the protest. 'They will deliver the numbers and will be a difficult force for any government to

ignore,' they intoned. 'Thondaman will be here at any moment, please place that question before him,' was my reply. However, I felt that in the first instance we must protest on our own without seeming to enlist the workers' support, which could be construed by the government as incitement and made into a political issue. I explained this to all those present.

Thondaman arrived, flanked by half a dozen deputies. I mentioned to him that the planters wanted his workers to join in the protest march to Colombo. "Do not expend all your ammunition in the first round of the battle," he said. "Make the protest and if the government does not pay heed to your warnings, I will take it forward from that point. However, I am giving you the assurance on the floor of this house that I will participate with you to the end, until we get this stopped." Knowing the trade union leader, that was good enough for all those gathered and it was decided to make the protest on our own.

Thondaman, in the meantime, called me aside and said that he had already informed the IGP of the catastrophic consequences that were bound to follow if the government went ahead with the scheme. "You go ahead with the march, the police will need to show the government that there is opposition and it is only then that they can caution the government to abandon the alienation." He had already set the stage for what was going to happen and also told them that if the government did not pay heed to representations made by the planters, he would oppose the land alienation. 'No surveyor will be allowed to come to the plantation and the next step would be an all-island strike,' he had warned the IGP. An all-island strike just before a general election would have been disastrous for those seeking re-election. We kept this protest outside politics. Thondaman was invited because he was the leading trade unionist in the area and not because he was a politician. A suggestion to invite Gamini Dissanayake to the meeting was not acceptable to us. Gamini, of course, would not have been unhappy at these developments!

A date was agreed upon for the march. It was to take place on

the May 24, 1977. The planters were all instructed to gather on the Galle Face Green and proceed from that point to the IGP's office. There was a lot of preparatory work to be done as well as meeting the media, giving them a comprehensive briefing on what was going on and why we were objecting to this scheme. It was also decided to meet the Deputy Inspector General of Police in charge of Colombo, to apprise him that the march was going to be quite peaceful and dignified, and that there would not be any untoward happenings. However, we decided to tell him that we would have no control over what would happen in the hill country if the government proceeded with the land acquisition.

Accordingly, we met the media at the Capri Club in Colombo and the Deputy Inspector General of Police at another location. From the body language of the policemen we were able to glean that they, too, considered this an irresponsible act just before a general election. In fact we were told that there would be no hindrance or harassment by the police and if we ran into any problem we should contact them. There were no mobile phones then but we were given an emergency police number.

This was the first time in the history of the planting profession that they were literally taking to the streets to prevent a reckless act by a desperate government. It was fraught with danger. The prime mover of the land take-over was Anura Bandaranaike, the son and heir of the Prime Minister, Mrs. Sirimavo Bandaranaike. If the government retained power we had no doubt that all of us would have had to pay a heavy price. In fact, messages were sent to us to refrain from the course of action decided upon. Again my mind went back to the Suicide Club. I was prepared to risk my job.

For a professional planter it is difficult to sit back and watch a plantation on which you have struggled to maintain the highest standards, ruined by haphazard and unplanned settlements. In fact we could already see the effects of land alienation on the few acres that were acquired some time back. The tea bushes were no more. We also understood in the clearest manner the inter-

The Galle Face Green - the launching pad of the protest march

community clashes that would take place if the land was given out. I, for one, did not oppose the alienation, but felt that it must be restricted to marginal lands and that the Tamil labour, too, should be given an opportunity to own land after a proper process of selection.

In addition to all of this, representatives of the labour force met us in their numbers and told us that it was clearly our duty to protect them and ensure that they got justice. 'We are prepared to do anything to prevent this. We don't need the trade unions, this is our land and we are prepared to fight for it.' In order to make the protest march effective, we needed the maximum participation of all the planters. The government could not take action against all the members of the planting community!

To me it will always be a sad tragedy that no government in office, including the present one, understands that the wealth of this country is in the plantations.

It was decided that I make the representations to the IGP. If we were to obtain a meeting with the Janatha Estates Development

Board and the State Plantations Corporation, it was Rodney De Mel who was to make the representations.

The day of May 24, dawned, and all of us were watching with apprehension the arrival and the participation of the planters. We realised that if there was no show of strength, the march would be a non-event. All our fears were allayed. We were receiving reports that the planters from the four corners of the island were all flocking in their numbers to the Galle Face Green. In addition to the planters, relatives, well wishers and others opposed to the land alienation were also arriving at the venue.

The Galle Face Green was a sea of heads. The plantation wives may have thought that this was a third world fashion parade as they were on the Green dressed in very elegant morning wear. Their presence added much-needed colour to the protest. They were not mere meek protesters either, and made their sentiments known quite vociferously. Some even offered to join us to meet the IGP. 'Poor bloody IGP,' said some of the husbands. 'What chance will he have with these women?' The ladies had to be gently told that this was not their show.

There was a strong police presence. A very senior officer, Assistant Superintendent of Police Rajapakse, approached us, flanked by a number of deputies and wanted to know what our intentions were. We told him that we were assembled on the Green to march to the Inspector General's office and that we proposed to do just that. The media was present and the cameras were clicking capturing this unusual planters' protest march for posterity. The planters were never associated with trade union action. A senior police officer was heard saying: 'These planters will teach the trade unionists a thing or two with the manner in which they have organised this event.'

A mobile police communication centre (com centre) was being operated from the Police Headquarters. The police were communicating with the IGP through the com centre:

Rajapakse: There are about 500 planters and their supporters along with their wives and well-wishers. They insist on marching to meet the IGP.

Police Headquarters: Are they causing any problems?

Rajapakse: No, Sir, this crowd is very orderly and disciplined. They are now assembling in a row and preparing to march to Police Headquarters. Some placards have come up and more people are joining the protesters.

Police Headquarters: Who are their leaders? Are they present?

The police walked up to us and wanted to know the names of the leaders. We gave them the names of Aelian De Silva, Rodney De Mel, P.H.A.N. Dias, and Herman Gunaratne.

After a period of silence, the radio crackled back to life.

Police Headquarters: Tell them the IGP will see their leaders and bring them to headquarters under escort. They have no permission for a demonstration so they cannot carry placards.

Rajapakse seemed to ignore the instructions of Police Headquarters and did not tell us to remove the placards. He somehow seemed to sense the mood of the moment and did not wish to cause any tension by asking us to remove them.

There was then a chorus of disappointment. The others were missing the fun. However, we advised them that we would accept the IGP's offer and meet him by ourselves.

We now assumed VIP status. The officers were extremely courteous and cooperative. We got into two or three vehicles and were taken under protected escort to the IGP's office.

We stopped on the way at the Bamboo Bar of the Grand Oriental Hotel as we were a little early. We had half an hour

before the appointment, which was just enough time to knock down a few gin and tonics!

At 10.30am we were ushered into the IGP's office. All the senior DIGs (Deputy Inspector Generals) were present, including S. P. Shanmugam of the Nuwara Eliya police. The presence of the senior policemen gave us a very clear message. They were taking us seriously. Some DIGs were our personal friends and they made light of the occasion by cracking a few jokes with us. 'These are past masters at this game. See how they have handled the media. This demonstration has attracted more media attention than any other dispute in the country,' one of them commented.

I outlined the case in very simple words. I had learnt that for any message to be effective it must be communicated in 10 minutes. If you take more than that you lose the attention of the listener. We told them of the dangerous situation developing on the plantations and that we would be holding the police responsible for any breach of the peace. I told them, "Please remember you cannot fight in the hills. You will not be allowed to enter the estates. The workers know how to fell trees and topple boulders to prevent police jeeps from coming anywhere near the plantations. You are allowing a situation to escalate out of control."

I continued: "You are the custodians of the Law. An election is just about to be held. No one knows the outcome. If there is a change of government, you, and you alone, will be held responsible to the new government for what has happened." From the body language it was clear that our message went home. They also knew that we were not without influence in the new government. S. P. Shanmugam perhaps knew a little more than he was prepared to divulge even to his superiors. He had information that we were quite close to J. R. Jayewardene, who may end up as the next Prime Minister. The police, too, were not unhappy to do us a few favours!

The IGP then addressed us, "I am meeting the Security

Council tomorrow. I will explain everything that you have told me to the political leaders. I will contact you tomorrow and let you know their decision." He went on to tell us to help maintain order and prevent a breach of the peace on the plantations. "We will try our best to resolve this matter," were his last words. It became quite evident to us that the police were fully aware of the situation and that they would ring the correct alarm bells. We were served with tea and short eats by the IGP after which we left Police Headquarters.

We returned to the Galle Face Green. The members were waiting for us anxiously. We gave them a briefing about our discussions. Privately I told them that I felt that the police would advise the politicians to be cautious about the land distribution.

The next day we met the heads of JEDB and SLSPC. The Chief of JEDB and son of the Governor General, Asoka Gopallawa, made a feeble attempt at arm twisting to which we reacted strongly. However, the head of the SLSPC and brother of the Prime Minister, Clifford Ratwatte, gave us the assurance that he would not allow any land to be distributed in this manner. "Don't tell this to the media. I will take suitable action to prevent this." We then realised that the government was backing down. We respected Clifford and did not mention this at the media briefing. The media men, however, knew that the land alienation was halted. 'Planters stop the Nuwara Eliya land alienation' screamed the morning papers in bold banner headlines. We had achieved our objective and returned back to the plantations after a merry weekend.

The shades of the Suicide Club again. We had gambled and won. The stakes were getting higher and higher!

The abortive land alienation gave me the signal to support the United National Party, led by J. R. Jayewardene. That was how I waded into the murky waters of Ceylon politics.

'For those who fight for it, life has a flavour that the sheltered will never know'

WE FIGHT THE GOVERNMENT OF THE DAY

'For those who fight for it, life has a flavour that the sheltered will never know'

The 1977 general election was won comprehensively by J. R. Jayewardene who went on to become the Prime Minister and later the first Executive President of Ceylon. I may have been naïve in the extreme and did not realise or understand that people take part in political campaigns to obtain prestigious positions for themselves. During the elections I addressed meetings in Kotmale and Nuwara Eliya in both Sinhala and Tamil. I was much sought after by the United National Party (UNP) because I was the friend of Thondaman, and he was playing a key role in the plantations, not only in Nuwara Eliya but throughout the whole country by delivering his vote bank to the UNP. He, himself, contested under the Cockerel, the symbol of the Ceylon Workers' Congress (CWC). There were some very interesting episodes during the campaign which made me realise that in politics, *no quarter is given, none asked.* Gamini Dissanayake, Thondaman and Anura Bandaranaike were contesting for power in the electorate. Gamini and Thondaman, though in an unannounced coalition, were competing in the same area for votes and each one was trying to outdo the other to obtain the biggest share of the preferential votes.

They were marching together but on separate roads. A letter was delivered from India about a week before the elections to every plantation worker. The gist of the letter, from the New Gandhian Society in India to the plantation workers, went as follows:

We, the New Gandhian Society, appeal to the plantation workers to vote for Gamini Dissanayake as it is he who can fulfil the aspirations of the Indian Tamil workers, and not Thondaman.

This letter was addressed to the workers from Tamil Nadu and bore the post mark of India. Almost 50,000 such letters were received. It seemed a very authentic document with an Indian

flag and a picture of the iconic Gandhi. This letter dealt a blow to Thondaman. He was livid with Gamini. In retaliation, he withdrew all the support for the UNP in the whole country. The UNP panicked. I was requested by Gamini, who, of course, denied the authorship of the letter, to meet Thondaman and request him to ignore this letter and support the party. "I did not get the letter written, somebody has done this to cause friction between us," was Gamini's story. A little thin, I thought, and told him so. "It is too late to argue about this, Herman. Meet your friend and somehow get him to continue supporting us. This is vital for our victory," he requested.

Thondaman was my friend and I could not tell him any lies. I was in a very difficult position and realised that Thondaman would doubt my *bona fides* if I went to him with a story as flimsy as this. At the same time, I knew that his support was vital for the UNP. I resolved to meet him. Thonda was using the holiday bungalow of UNP Minister M. H. Mohamed as his campaign headquarters. There was a big crowd round him. He appeared to be giving an interview to Mark Tully, the BBC correspondent in Delhi, who was covering Ceylon from India. He greeted me warmly and told me that he would like to meet me on a very urgent matter after his interview with Mark Tully. He introduced me to Tully as an old friend and sat down to the interview.

This is how the interview went:

Mark Tully: Mr. Thondaman, you are the leader of the main workers' trade union in the plantations. Are you contesting with the UNP?

Thondaman: No. I am contesting under the flag of the CWC and my symbol is the cockerel. The UNP symbol is the elephant.

Mark Tully: In the other areas outside Nuwara Eliya-Maskeliya, are you supporting the UNP?

Thondaman: My voters will decide whom I should support after the elections.

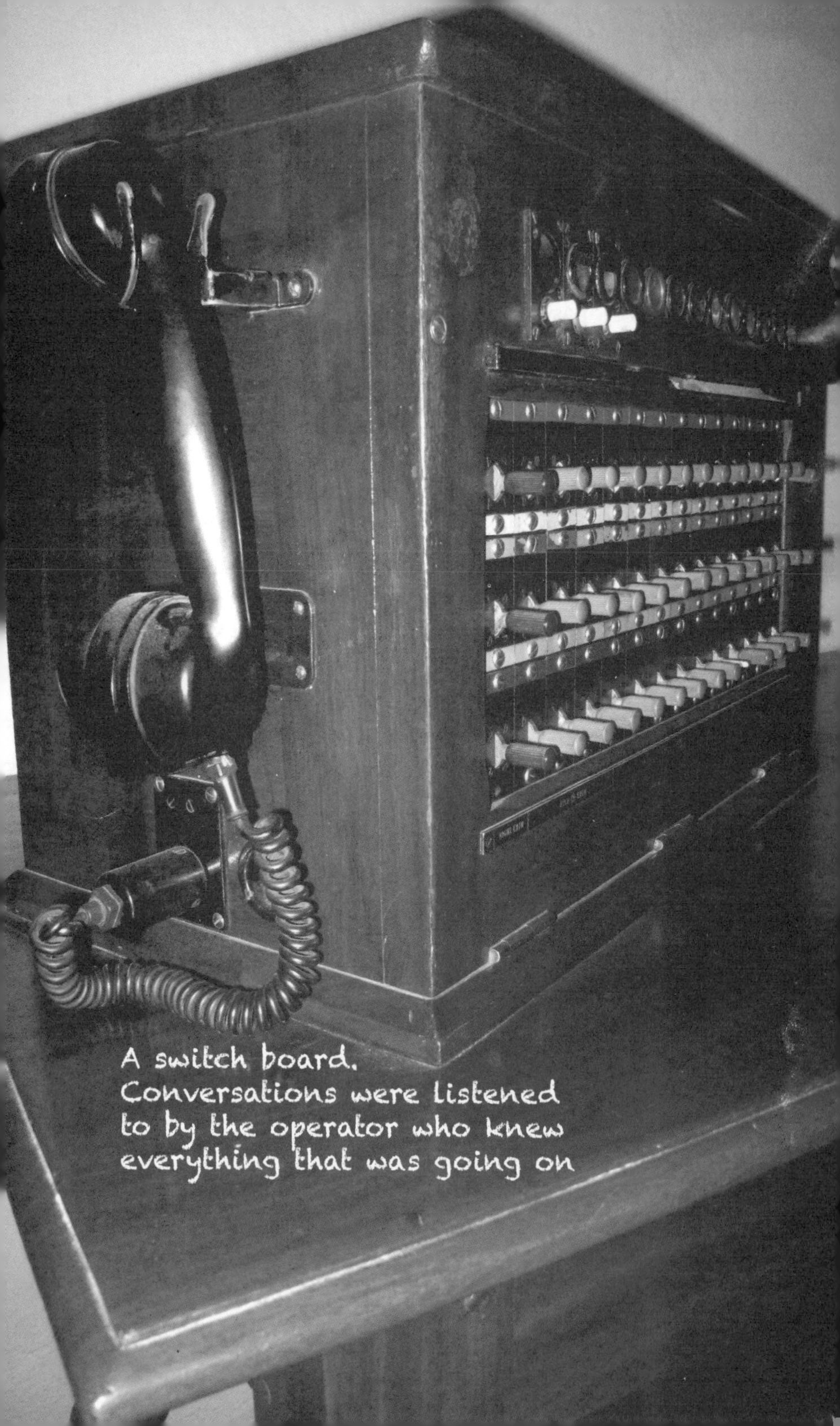

A switch board.
Conversations were listened to by the operator who knew everything that was going on

Mark Tully: Do you have an agreement with the UNP to support them after the elections?

Thondaman: No. I have no such agreement.

Mark Tully: Then do you have a secret agreement to support the UNP?

Thondaman: What arrr (he rolls his R's) you talking about? If I have a secret agreement, it is a secret, no? I am not going to tell you. (Laughing) Why arrr you asking me?

Tully was bowled over by this man and later told me that he was one of the smartest politicians that he had met in the sub-continent.

Thondaman retired to his office and asked me to join him. He was going to take up the question of the letter from India. "See what this Gamini is doing? He has sent this letter to every one of my members and they truly believe it to be from the Indian leaders. I have no time to go round the electorate and tell them that this is a bogus letter and they may all vote for Gamini," he said, waving the letter at me. "He has tricked me. I have no alternative but to withdraw all support for the UNP. I have a clear understanding with JR. I don't blame JR for this letter. This is all Gamini's work. I don't think JR knows that a trick like this has been played on me." I did not interrupt him, nor did I give him any excuses for the letter.

I told him, however, that he could easily use his district representatives to inform the plantation workers to ignore the letter. In the meantime, he had withdrawn all his campaign staff from the entire island to the Nuwara Eliya district to beef up his flagging campaign. After a great deal of persuasion and spending almost three hours, I was able to obtain his continued support. This was after I slipped out of his campaign headquarters, spoke to J. R. Jayewardene and got him to talk to Thondaman. JR apologised to Thondaman and told him that he would get the CID to investigate this matter after he won the elections, and then take suitable action.

After speaking to JR, Thondaman came back and told me, "He is pleading with me not to withdraw support, saying that a CID investigation will be initiated to find out who sent this letter. What is the use? The damage is already done. An investigation after the elections has no meaning. I will not go back on my word. I will continue to support the UNP, but tell Gamini not to do dirty things like this."

Thondaman was too much of a realist. He was not going to allow an incident like this to alter his national stance. JR, too, realised that Thondaman was a firm and steadfast friend. Thondaman later used this incident to his advantage and was able to obtain some significant demands and concessions on behalf of the plantation workers.

I went back to Gamini and told him that, at least for the moment, the problem appeared to be settled. "You should not make use of this letter now," I said. He smiled mischievously and left little doubt in my mind about the origins of the letter from India!

It is necessary for the reader to understand Thondaman. He was a rich landowner who could have lived a life of luxury. Instead he saw the appalling conditions under which the plantation workers lived and chose to espouse their cause. He was the single most powerful man in this island. He had total control over 500,000 workers. They did exactly as he told them. No party in Ceylon could have attained political power without his support. He used this power to extract all the advantages for his people. He was the Messiah of the workers. It was my good fortune to have him as a close personal friend.

The campaign in Nuwara Eliya which had turned into a veritable battle ground, swung into high gear. A bitter fight for power ensued. JR himself campaigned for Gamini and

Peering into the past
from the house where
the Suicide Club met

Thondaman. When he was in the Nuwara Eliya District, his headquarters were at Pem's bungalow on Sheen Group. I accompanied him for some meetings and was able to get a full measure of this freedom fighter.

Many are the stories he told us about the old days and the struggle for freedom. He understood the people of Ceylon very well, he knew of their hopes and aspirations. However, he never played to the gallery. I can still remember going with him to a political rally in Kotmale. We passed many villages and came to a particularly lonely spot which was nevertheless close to the meeting ground. He saw a Sinhala villager quite oblivious to the activity going on in the area, seated on a rock and scratching his what-you-may-call-them nonchalantly, if not insolently. JR saw this spectacle and nudged me. "Can you see that man and what he is doing? He is most unconcerned about our meeting and what is going on in the area. As long as there are people like that, this country we will never go communist!" he opined.

JR never spoke for more than 10 minutes. He told me that if you cannot get a message across within that time, the message has no value. On the way to this meeting, he saw a small boy rolling an empty reel of thread on a stick, making a noise as if he were driving a car. I could see him observing this boy with grave attention.

When the leader arrived at a meeting he was given the opportunity to speak as he had to attend several other meetings. This was what he said: "I have attended and addressed over 100 large rallies like this in the country and I have absolutely no doubt that the UNP will form the next government. I will be the Prime Minister. On the way to this meeting I saw a small boy rolling an empty reel of thread on a stick. He was also making a noise as if he were driving a car. This symbolises our backward country. Children in the West are playing with computer driven cars and engaging in highly technical computer games. Our children are playing

with reels of thread and pieces of stick. A child is a child anywhere in the world. I am going to give our children the same opportunities as the children in the West."

This message went home because it connected immediately with the people. I thought to myself how cleverly this man used what he had observed a little while ago so as to reach out to them and strike a chord.

To me, moving around with him was such a stimulating experience. He packed a box of sandwiches when he was on the campaign trail, ate his frugal meal under a tree, folded the piece of paper in which he had wrapped his sandwiches and placed it back in the box for disposal in a dustbin. He had a perfect sense of humour, and could take the tension off a difficult moment with light-hearted banter.

He had great hopes for his country. In my opinion he made the biggest contribution to the economic development of modern Ceylon. Born in an era where agitation was by *satyagraha* and peaceful placard waving and slogan shouting, he did not understand terrorism. He was to pay the price for this later.

We discussed Machiavelli, Alexander the Great, politics and the general state of the plantations. I was not in the habit of telling people what they liked to hear.as I was trained to be frank and open

THE MORE THINGS CHANGE......

J. R. Jayewardene won a convincing and resounding victory and he was sworn in as the Prime Minister.

Pem Seneviratne, my friend and neighbour on Sheen Group was appointed the Chairman of the Janatha Estates Development Board (JEDB). He became one of the most powerful men in the country. I resigned to continue working on Dunsinane as the Manager. I was of course hopeful that the new government would not practice the same nepotism as the previous one. The Prime Minister made some very good appointments and gave a clear signal to the country that he was going to govern the land properly. This was a welcome change from the past.

Pem later appointed me as the Regional Manager for Nuwara Eliya. This was the largest and the best tea district in the island. I was in charge of almost 100,000 acres of Ceylon's best tea lands. I was 33 years of age, the youngest to hold this position.

This was also the first political appointment in my career. However, I refused to relinquish my substantive position as Manager of Dunsinane. Deep down within me I probably realised that I would not last in a position where I had to be answerable to others. I resolved to do my best in this new and exciting assignment. This was quite an important position, as I had to look after all visiting dignitaries, political leaders and Heads of State when they visited Nuwara Eliya, the showpiece hill resort of the British Empire.

I was functioning as the Chief Executive. This work would normally have been done by two agency houses with about two dozen senior directors, executives, accountants, tea tasters and a battery of trained personnel.

In addition to the bungalow on Dunsinane, I also had an official residence in Nuwara Eliya, the Summerhill Bungalow. This was large and sprawling, with manicured lawns and about six bedrooms. However, I chose to occupy Dunsinane bungalow. Official visitors were entertained at Summerhill.

This later became a nuisance to me. Since it was not occupied, many of the country's most powerful politicians started asking me for Summerhill for the April holidays. The first outsider to whom I gave the bungalow was the Minister of Finance. He enjoyed my hospitality and made some regrettable statements at a subsequent Cabinet meeting, which got me into trouble. I am going to relate this story just to illustrate the complexities of political appointments and of breaking bread with politicians.

One Sunday morning I received a call from Gamini Dissanayaka, who was, by then, the Minister of Irrigation, Power and Highways. It was the most powerful ministry in the country.

"Herman," he said after exchanging a few pleasantries, "your kinsman, the Minister of Finance is cooped up in a room at the General's House (the holiday residence of Members of Parliament) in Nuwara Eliya with his wife and family. He is useful to me. He called me a little while ago, asking me whether I could find him more comfortable accommodation." Gamini knew that I was not occupying the Summerhill bungalow and asked me if I could allow the Minister to stay in it for a few days.

This is the mistake I made. "Yes, it can be done," I told him.

"Can you then go to the General's house and rescue him from his predicament and install him at the Summerhill Bungalow?" he asked.

I agreed to do this. What I should have done was simply to say that the bungalow was occupied by some overseas visitors and that would have been the end of the story. In hindsight, I regret not having said so. It caused a problem not only for me but also for my Minister M. D. H. Jayawardena, one of the most refined members of the cabinet.

When I arrived at the General's house the Finance Minister and his family were visibly relieved to see me. Their bags were all packed and they were in the small, poky little sitting room awaiting my arrival. I went to the bedroom with the Finance Minister to organise the transfer of his baggage and was surprised at what I saw.

The room was extremely small. We could have put three of those rooms into a plantation bungalow bedroom. I did not know if the daughter and son-in-law had another room. I thought to myself, 'Why on earth did this man accept all this discomfort?' He could easily have gone to the best hotel in Nuwara Eliya. He was not deficient in the cash department! On the contrary, he was well off.

His whole family was very charming and solicitous with me. No wonder, since I had rescued them!

I duly installed them in my official residence and gave instructions to the staff to look after the Ministerial party and to treat them well. Just before I left, I gave the keys of the liquor cabinet to the wife of the Minister and told her to keep them in her custody, as the plantation cooks could be trusted with most things, but when it came to liquor, they were not averse to knocking down a few bottles and filling them with water to maintain the original levels!

The Finance Minister invited me to dinner the next day. I gladly accepted. He was an extremely clever man, had many academic qualifications and was a Classics scholar in school. I was looking forward to an interesting evening. Classics and learning, I thought, gave a man a certain refinement and culture.

The next day I arrived at the bungalow and sat down to a few drinks in the evening. The conversation was quite stimulating. We discussed Machiavelli, Alexander the Great, politics and the general state of the plantations. I was not in the habit of telling people what they liked to hear as I was trained to be frank and open.

During the course of the conversation he asked me, "Herman, how are you running the plantations?" I told him that we had an acute shortage of trained staff. I was, after

all, doing the work of two agency houses and to service the plantations properly we needed to have efficient staff. I further told him that I was endeavouring to obtain some good personnel from the plantations in the area to assist me in the regional office.

He then asked me my views on the nationalisation of the plantation sector. My reply was that politics and political appointments must not permeate the plantations and that the manager of an estate must be given all the support and freedom to perform his duties without any outside intervention. He then asked me, "What do you think of privatising the plantations?" My reply was that a vibrant private sector besides the state-managed plantations would be good for both as there would then be a basis of comparative evaluation of their efficiency. I realised that the Finance Minister was thinking of a way of giving the plantations back to the private sector. I thought this was in the best interests of the plantations, to have the private sector and the public sector competing vibrantly to obtain the best results. I realised much later that I should have been a little more cautious in what I told him.

He was extremely demanding during his stay. When a pipeline of water to the bungalow was disrupted, the Finance Minister telephoned the nearest plantation manager and insisted that he attended to it immediately and personally. The Manager who was contacted saw this as an opportunity to ingratiate himself with the Finance Minister and was seen visiting the Summerhill bungalow daily, simply to ensure that the party had water for their daily bath. The manager sweated to ensure that they bathed!

Politicians love this obsequious servility. The Manager (the pipeline supervisor) got himself invited to dinner. He was a very senior man, and counted about 25 years more planting experience than I had. He may also have been a little envious of a junior guy like me running the plantations. He and his wife were the best entertainers when it came to organising a dinner party. His tableware and presentation would have made the Mossops look like poor relatives in the dinner party business! The Finance Minister was wined and dined!

Many planters in the area passed on this information to me. It did not bother me in the least as I was not in the entertainment business. I would rather have had my string hoppers in the comparative comfort of my sarong rather than dress up for these formal dinners! The visiting Minister entertained other less fortunate politicians who had also arrived in Nuwara Eliya during the season at the Summerhill bungalow. He was laying it on thick!

April came and passed. I suddenly got a call from Gamini Dissanayake. "Herman," he said, "the Finance Minister said some very unpleasant things about you and the plantations at the cabinet meeting today. I was a little shocked, as it was at my request that you gave him your bungalow. What kind of guy is he to have enjoyed your hospitality and then make statements like this to the Cabinet?"

A thin veneer of civility does not always mask congenital coarseness, I thought.

Gamini then went on to tell me what the Minister had said at the Cabinet meeting. He had mentioned no names but left no doubt

The caps did not always fit

in anyone's mind about whom he was referring to: 'I was at a senior Regional Manager's bungalow. Nothing has changed in the Plantation Raj. The liquor cabinets are full of the choicest wines. They say they are not running the plantations properly. That they do not have trained staff and that there is political interference in a big way. The regional manager also said that the plantations would be better off if they were privatised.' The reader may well wonder if this self-righteous man left my liquor cabinet untouched. It was not quite empty but he had given a good account of himself in the free liquor department!

I told Gamini what actually transpired. He gave me the inside story of what led to this harangue from the minister. 'You know the Finance Minister and the Minister of Plantation Industries, the Hon. M. D. H. Jayawardena, are having a running battle. MDH is a thoroughly honourable man and this fellow is always interfering in the affairs of the Plantation Ministry as he claims he knows more than anyone else about plantations having inherited an estate as a dowry from his wife. He does not miss an opportunity to take a shot at MDH.' This was no consolation to me as I knew then that this was not going to end there. I told Gamini that all this happened because we gave Summerhill to him. He agreed with me and stated that

never would he ask me to give the bungalow to anyone again.

As expected, I was summoned to Colombo by the Plantation Minister, M. D. H. Jayawardena. The summons came through Bradman Weerakoon, the Secretary to the Ministry. I had great respect for Bradman and I knew that he, too, liked me. Bradman Weerakoon belonged to the old school civil service and he was Secretary to three previous Prime Ministers. He was an extremely polished and amiable man. Both of us went to the same school, as did the Minister who caused this problem. I remembered that '*One swallow never made a summer.*' The Minister's reputation was known to all. Having been briefed by Gamini immediately after the cabinet meeting, I knew the reason for the summons.

Bradman met me in his room and was extremely courteous. "Herman," he said, "the Minister is very upset about what you told the Finance Minister and also for giving him one of our bungalows without our Minister's knowledge." I listened to Bradman. He repeated what Gamini told me. I explained to him at length what transpired and told him that everything I had said had been twisted round, misrepresented and distorted. I further told him the story of the liquor cabinet. I told him that this liquor was purchased to entertain official and overseas visitors who came on business to the Nuwara Eliya region and that although I was entitled to, I never took them to hotels or clubs but entertained them at Summerhill. Bradman knew this because he had stayed at Summerhill and had enjoyed his stay while conducting himself with great dignity and decorum.

"Why on earth did you give him the keys to the liquor cabinet? These are the matters that could be held against you, especially when you work for the public sector." I apologised to him for what had happened and said that I was just going out of my way to be hospitable to the Finance Minister. I further told him that it was Gamini who was trying to help him out of an accommodation problem in Nuwara Eliya. Having got my side of the story he took me to the Minister.

MDH was angry with me. "Why did you give that fellow the bungalow? Our bungalows must not be given to anybody, other than our own people, without reference to me!" he told me somewhat angrily. I remained silent.

Bradman Weerakoon then intervened and told him the full story. "Sir, Herman is quite a reliable guy, I know him well and what he has stated has been misrepresented. He would never let the side down. He is one of our very top people." I then apologised to my Minister and told him that this was an unanticipated consequence of my trying to accommodate the Finance Minister, and that it would never happen again.

"Don't take this too seriously. I know that fellow, and he is always trying to find fault with the plantations. He should mind his own business without interfering. In future, don't ever give him our bungalows. Let him stay wherever he likes. If a request is made to you, tell them that you cannot give out estate bungalows without reference to me and refer the matter to Bradman. I trust you, and know you are loyal to me," M. D. H. Jayawardena reassured me. "Don't let this affect your work. The matter is over and I will handle the Finance Minister on this issue." I went back to my home relieved, but having learnt an important lesson.

'*Some people look at a gift horse in the mouth.*'

The best teas in the world,
anywhere in the world, are
made when the climate is at
its driest and the temperatures
are at their lowest. This is an
indisputable fact. Dry weather
causes a concentration in the
sap content and brings about
certain desirable features
called flavour, pungency and
quality (these are seasonal
factors) used to describe
exceptional teas

BEFORE AND AFTER WE CONFOUND THE CRITICS

I was fully absorbed in my job as the Regional Manager of Nuwara Eliya. Though I continued as Manager of Dunsinane, this was only nominally so. My Senior Assistant, Ravi Kotelawala, functioned as the *de facto* Manager.

I was able to ward off the political interventions on the plantations as I knew all the politicians. However, I realised that they were the representatives of the people and had to be accommodated wherever possible. This was not difficult to do, if you did not allow yourself to be intimidated by them. I held the view that the politician was a part and parcel of the system. After all, the plantations belonged to the state and it is the politician who looks after the hopes and aspirations of the people. Not a single one of them made any unreasonable demands. They had access to me at any time and I went out of my way to assist them when they came to me with their problems.

We ran the plantations to the best of our ability. In hindsight, I must say that the plantations were far better run in that era by the state, than today after privatisation. It was always my belief that '*Management is the development of people and not the direction of things*' (Peter Drucker, an American Management expert). I sought to recruit like-minded managers to run the Regional Office. My first choice was Anura Gunasekera, a long-time friend and the Manager of Eskdale Estate, Kandapola. Anura was an upright man who was a very competent planter. He had an excellent sense of humour and could be completely depended upon. He was seconded from his job on Eskdale.

I also wanted a good Tea Manufacturing Advisor. The obvious choice was Ralston Tissera, a very successful tea-maker. Ralston had a feel for a tea factory. He could walk in and, within minutes, work out what was going on. He did this sometimes straight from the Golf Club after a heavy night's drinking! He was considered an eccentric and I was warned that he was difficult to work with. I had no such problem with him and he became my steadfast friend, even during bad times.

Ceylon is a magical island. The wealth of our country, I always maintained, was in the manicured plantations, the most enduring legacy left behind for us by the British Empire. I never ceased to marvel at the magnificent infrastructure the British had built. They also set some norms and reached some conclusions which everybody accepted because they were told so. I was determined to break this mould.

The most amazing feature about our country is that the climate zones change within a few hours, if not minutes. I am going to tell you a tantalising story of how we used the climate zones to break some permanently accepted norms and principles of tea manufacture.

I will try to explain the technicalities as it is important for the reader to understand exactly what we did. Within the Nuwara Eliya region there were three distinct climate zones: Nuwara Eliya was one: Uda Pusellawa was another: Radella and Agrapatna were listed together and called the Dimbulas. These three sub-districts made very, very distinct teas.

It was considered impossible for one district to make a tea with the character of another climate zone. In fact, teas from the same sub-district differ from factory to factory. Such are the complexities of tea manufacturing. There are a thousand permutations and configurations to the production of the tea. The type of tea bush, the age of the plantation, the type of fertiliser applied, the pest control methods used, the situation of the factory, and the direction of the wind are some of the features that influence the manufacture of tea. Seedling tea would make a better liquor than the higher-yielding, vegetatively-propagated material.

The best teas in the world, anywhere in the world, are

made when the climate is at its driest and the temperatures are at their lowest. This is an indisputable fact. Dry weather causes a concentration in the sap content and brings about certain desirable features called flavour, pungency and quality which are seasonal factors used to describe exceptional teas and are not present throughout the year. These are tea-making terms which identify the smallest nuance in the production of a tea. Quality is seasonal and a desirable feature; flavour is pronounced; and quality and pungency (astringency) is quality plus flavour.

These desirable characteristics of a tea depend on the time of year and are completely weather-related. The older the tea bush, the better the quality. The same principles, I am told, apply to making wine. Tea making is exactly like that. Certain regions in France make a wine that cannot be duplicated by any other region. So it is with tea.

The best teas in the Highlands (over an elevation

The day's labour entered in the pass book

of 4000 feet) are made in the Uva District. No plantation on the island had been able to come near the prices obtained by the estates in the Uva region. It was an accepted fact. Nobody tried to do differently since it was considered impossible. The Uva District was not within my area of control.

However, the plantations in the Uda Pusellawa region were under my purview. Uda Pusellawa had similar climatic conditions to Uva. The top quality tea manufacturing season in Uva starts in June and goes on until August. This is the time that the *Kachan* winds blow across the plantations from the Eastern Province of the island. It is the *Kachan* wind that plays on the tea bush and concentrates the sap rapidly, bringing about these desirable aspects. Intense *Kachan* winds hit the Uva first, and winds of less intensity blow across the Uda Pusellawa zone.

Kolitha Ratnayaka was the General Manager of JEDB. He asked me casually one day, "Herman, is there any reason that you cannot make as good a tea in the Uda Pussellawa range similar to the teas made in the Uva?"

I replied that this was possible but we had to convince the managers that it could be done.

"Let's do it. You are the best man for the job of convincing people," he averred.

This was a tall order. Not because I thought it was impossible, but because I realised that human achievement first starts in the mind of man, and that we had to convince the managers in Uda Pusellawa that it could be done. I discussed this with my colleagues Anura and Ralston in the regional office."This is worth striving for," I said, adding, "it has never ever happened in the long history of the plantations but I feel that we can do it."

Anura and Ralston both agreed. I requested them to invite the brokers to Nuwara Eliya to take this forward. All the brokers came in response to my invitation. However, I

realised that they were wondering if we had 'bats in the belfry' to think of such an impossible scheme.

We had to convince the brokers first. After all, these were the guys who sold the tea. Our plan was in fact quite simple. The strategy arose as a consequence of the distilled essence of my discussions with Anura and Ralston.

All we had to do was to simulate the climatic conditions of Uva in Uda Pusellawa. Uva made pungent flavours. We had the potential to make light, bright (reference to the liquor) teas with very delicate flavours. We then told the brokers how this could be done. Most of them expressed their views and told us clearly that they did not think this was ever going to be possible. International buyers came down to Ceylon especially for the Uva season and competed fiercely for the Uva teas. They had got used to the Uva liquors.

Some leading London brokers visited Ceylon. When we outlined what we were attempting to do they articulated their views very frankly: that 'it had never happened before and that it was unlikely to happen then.' However, they told us to send them some early samples by air mail so that they could report on the teas within 10 days and let us know what they thought of our progress.

All teas were sold through the Colombo auctions. The tea tasters received samples of the current manufacture and they evaluated and tasted the teas, and made their bids on the floor of the Auction House.

If a special tea was observed, they air mailed the sample to prospective buyers in London, France, Japan and Russia. If the buyer liked the tea he sent an air mail bid to the auction floor through his agent in Colombo. Nobody knew the limit of this bid other than the representative of the buyer in Colombo. Sometimes it was known that they gave an open ended bid. 'Buy this tea at any price. Have a tape recorder at the auction just to ensure that there is competitive bidding and no price fixing.' The auction system in Ceylon was completely transparent. It was the duty of the brokers to find out if there was any interest *via* air mail on a tea before the auction. This was like peeping into your opponent's hand in a card game of poker. If you knew beforehand that there was an airmail bid, you asked for a high starting price and within seconds an experienced seller (broker) would know from the nature of the bids coming in and the body language of the bidder that the particular tea was going through the roof. Competing buyers would not allow a good tea to be sold cheap. If we knew that an airmail bid was received, we made arrangements from a friendly buyer to put in a few aggressive bids!

I studied the nuances in the marketplace and made arrangements to send the good samples well in time to the brokers, and sometimes direct to the buyers, so that they, in turn, could send off the samples by airmail quickly. All this was worked out beforehand. Ralston was in complete charge of this operation. Anura was handling the brokers and the buyers, and supervising the dispatch of samples.

We summoned a meeting of the managers in the Uda Pusellawa area and gave them a good motivational talk. This meeting was held well before the flavoury season so that everyone involved could get their act together in good time. The plantation Manager who got the highest price was offered a holiday to the value of Rs.5000.

Pem Seneviratne, JEDB Chairman, agreed to this, knowing full well, perhaps, that the Rs.5000 was safe and that no one was going to get this reward. This was still a very handsome sum in those days, where managers could not afford to spend Rs.5000 on a family holiday. We also impressed upon them the need to maintain confidentiality about our plans. We were going to take the Uva estates on the blind side!

Ralston then took the floor and advised them on how this could be achieved. "Manufacture only the old field leaf.

Get the green leaf to the factory fast. Have four or even five weighings a day. Do not damage or crush the leaf. As the leaf comes into the factory spread it on the troughs. Do not spread the leaf too thick on the troughs. Start the withering immediately. Remember the leaf is already half withered on the bush itself due to the *Kachchan* winds. Take a slightly soft wither and the moment the leaf is ready, start the rolling or 'rotorvaning' (leaf maceration) process. Fermentation may or may not be necessary as the outside temperature is high," he said.

During the flavoury season the teas were usually manufactured at night. Ralston did not agree with this. "Start when the wither is ready even if it is three o'clock in the afternoon. Manufacture one batch and if the wither is not ready on the other batches, stop and restart. The main thing is to start the manufacture when the wither is ready. The wither, next to the standard of leaf, is the most critical factor in tea making," he explained. Ralston held nothing back. He gave them the benefit of his 30 years as Ceylon's top tea-making Superintendent.

Slowly, realisation dawned on the managers present that we had all of this worked out. Indeed, they understood that it could be done. Ralston told the planters that he would be available at any time of the day or night for consultations. He further told them that they must have regular tea tasting sessions in the factory itself, so that the progress could be evaluated then and there. "I will be visiting every factory in the Uda Pusellawa area throughout this period. I will not be able to give you notice of my visit, as I, myself will not know where I will be. If I find that suitable conditions exist on a particular plantation at a particular time, I will be there. If you have other work, don't bother to be in attendance. I will handle the manufacture with the Factory Officer." Saying so he laid out the ground rules clearly.

Anura Gunasekera was handling the dispatch of samples

and was also liaising with the brokers and buyers. He was very courteous, highly polished, and had a very special way of getting the job done. He was not very good at entertaining any excuses from anybody for whatever reason. He carried his outstanding physique and personality with unassuming charm though it would most certainly have persuaded others to take him seriously!

These men were but a few, but they were the best.

The planters left the meeting full of enthusiasm. Determination was visible. One or two of them came up to me and said, "Chief, don't worry, we will deliver the goods." Anura, Ralston and I met after the meeting. We agreed that we had succeeded in firing their imagination to go for it.

The flavoury season begins when the direction of the wind starts changing. This can happen at any time during the month of June - sometimes a little early or sometimes a little late. Ralston was monitoring the wind currents and the ambient temperatures together with the hygrometric differences. These were essential features in the production of top flavour.

He visited the plantations well before the season began to get to know the staff in the factories and to prime them for the challenge ahead. The plantations were ready for the event. There was an all-pervading and heightened sense of anticipation. It was the passion that we were trying to create - the passion to excel.

The season finally arrived. We soon realised that the objective we were seeking to achieve was possible. The initial reaction from the Colombo and London brokers was excellent. 'We have never seen teas like this from Uda Pussellawa,' and other similar statements were the responses we got. We knew that we were going to make it.

At the first flavoury season auction, Brookside Estate, managed by Vinnie Boteju got Rs.72 per kilo. No Uva

estate was able to equal this. At the next sale, St. Leonards, managed by Yasa Ratnayaka achieved Rs.94 per kilo for a line of BOP. Nothing from Uva came close.

At the last quality sale Harold Ratwatte from Luckyland created an all-time record for a BOP at Rs.104 per kilo. No Uva plantation was able to come anywhere near these prices.

Many other estates also got better prices than Uva could come up with. Kirklees got a Rs.62 per kilo sale and Delmar obtained Rs.65 per kilo.

We had, by now, comprehensively beaten and even surpassed the Uva estates.

The tea industry, in its 150 year history had never seen this performance. That was in 1978. Today, 32 years later (in 2010), not one estate, including those in Uda Pusellawa has been able to repeat this achievement.

This was a collective effort by the team that we put together. I never visited a factory during this time. I was quite content to leave the action in the hands of the men who were doing the job. It was a remarkable occurrence and many writers on the history of tea have dealt with this.

Harold got his Rs.5000 holiday. This was by no means a personal triumph. I had very little to do with it other than getting a highly motivated team to achieve the impossible.

'*Whatsoever man can conceive in his mind, he can also achieve.*'

You go round
the world but
you come back
to the land of
your forefathers.
'For the ashes
of your fathers
and the temples
of your gods'

RETURN TO THE RUHUNA

You retire only when you die. You die when you retire, not once, but so many times if you have time on your hands with nothing to do.

The planter's real trauma begins when he leaves the plantations at 55 years of age and starts the life of retirement. Planters have very little savings. Most of them buy small houses in Colombo and resign themselves to a life of reading the newspapers in the morning and visiting children and grandchildren during the day. They have to buy themselves a small car and live on their savings, which are quite insignificant at today's cost of living. The bigger trauma is to get permanently used to small houses with much smaller rooms, and tiny patches of garden, without domestic staff, having had half a dozen of them on the plantation. Life was so good on the estates that you never thought of retirement till the day finally crept up on you, like a thief in the night.

My British colleagues, some of whom I have met in later years, went through this same traumatic experience. To them, there was no place like Ceylon, and they talked about it nostalgically. Most of them, given half a chance, would have loved to return to the place which was their second home. Some of them did indeed return to play out their last days on this magical island.

I was determined not to ride into the twilight and a life of retirement. Retirement is a word that is somehow totally unacceptable to me. You have to die on your feet.

I must crave the reader's indulgence to talk about how I faced the period when the shadows began to lengthen for me. The story is mine, not because it is marked by some great achievements, but simply because nobody likes to talk about life after the plantations. After the glory days.

Since leaving the plantations, I have had many stimulating, and some harrowing experiences. I was the General Manager of the country's most ambitious development scheme since gaining independence: the development of the Mahaweli River

basin. This appointment resulted in my having to spend a short spell in solitary confinement, and later under house arrest when I had to face the wrath of the government of the day (this episode is dealt with in my book *For A Sovereign State*).

I was rescued by my friend the Hon. S. Thondaman who appointed me as a Chairman of one of his Corporations, dealing with the development of the handloom industry on the island. After two years I was sacked in 24 hours by the then President, Ranasinghe Premadasa.

I had to return to Ruhuna. My maternal grandfather, K.C. Albert De Silva of Matara, was an extremely wealthy man who owned around 3000 acres of land in Ruhuna.

The story of my grandfather must be told, not so much because of his enormous wealth, but because of some of the things that he did, which resulted in him losing his fortune. It is also an interesting story that speaks eloquently and dramatically about how enormous fortunes can be lost. Overnight.

My grandfather married Nalini, a girl from the Jayawickema family. There were 14 members in this large family. One brother, Sargo Jayawickrama was an All-Ceylon cricket captain, a splendid cricketer in his day and likened to Sir Wally Hammond of England. Another was Dio Jayawickerema, a Queen's Counsel appointed by Her Majesty the Queen of England. Another brother was a judge of the Supreme Court and yet another was a very senior lawyer, who later became a judge. The other girls married men of distinction, who later produced sons of very great eminence and learning.

One of the sons of the Jayawickrema clan needs special mention. He was Dr. Raja De Silva who later went on to become the Commissioner of Archaeology. He is the man who debunked the story of the famous Sigiriya Rock Fortress.

Sigiriya is Ceylon's greatest monument to her rich and advanced heritage. It was a rock fortress built by a parricide King Kassapa after he assassinated his father, King Dhatusena.

Today, Sigiriya stands as a scarred and lonely sentinel, rising majestically to the sky. It bears mute testimony to an ancient civilisation, withstanding the pitiless march of time. This was a magical and romantic story related in the folklore of the land. Dr. Raja, by very learned and substantiated presentations, established clearly that it was a Mahayana monastery and not the rock fortress of the parricide King. He has written many books on Sigiriya.

It was Albert De Silva who eventually bequeathed to me the lands on which I earn my living now. He was 39 years old when he passed away to meet his Maker. He was born to a life of luxury. His father had a fleet of ships and was the supplier of rice to the British Army. He led an amazing life during the British period and was driven around in a Rolls Royce car by an English chauffeur!

My grandfather was a President of the Suicide Club. The Suicide Club was restricted to the elite of Ceylon society, and as if that were not enough, every member had to have with him, all the time, Rs.25,000 on his person. Whenever they met, which was most evenings, they played a card game called 'Asking Hitting.'

He was a very gentle man - courteous and soft spoken, well mannered and attired in the most fashionable clothes of that time. Many tried to dissuade him from the gambling habit, without much success. All the lands were registered in his name. The deeds were in the possession of my grandmother as it was she who looked after all his properties.

One day, playing a game of cards, he lost heavily at the table. He had exhausted all the money on his person, and he ran up a debt of Rs.90,000. This was an extremely tidy sum of money at that time. Gambling debts had to be settled within 48 hours. That was the unwritten rule of the Suicide Club. Even to commit suicide they had rules!

He did not have the ready cash to settle this debt. He had come to my grandmother and asked her for the deeds of Edunkele Estate. She was not about to give him the deeds and had questioned why he wanted them. He reluctantly told her the story of the gambling debt and that the money had to be settled in 48 hours.

She panicked and immediately contacted her brothers who were leading members of the legal profession. Their advice was that the debt could be settled in a couple of weeks and that there was no need to sell Edunkele Estate. Although there was no legal obligation to pay a gambling debt, there was no doubt that he would settle the debt of honour or that he would abdicate his responsibility. Not even my grandmother's brother, Dio Jayawickrama QC, ever contemplated not paying - and he only advised that taking a little time to settle would be quite in order. Albert De Silva, however, insisted that he had to settle his dues in 48 hours, according to the unwritten rule of the Suicide Club!

To have been a gambler is to leave a permanent stigma on your life. To honour your debts even at the gambling table and walk away as if nothing has happened symbolises the virtues of standing by your word. K. C. Albert De Silva was such a man. The poem *If* by Rudyard Kipling symbolises the character of my grandfather.

Herman's grandfather President of the Suicide Club K.C.Albert De Silva

If you can make
one heap of
all your winnings
And risk it on
one turn of pitch-and-toss,
And lose, and start again
at your beginnings.
And never breathe a word
about your loss;
If you can force
your heart and nerve and sinew
To serve your turn
long after they are gone,
And so hold on
when there is nothing in you
Except the Will which says to them: "Hold on!"

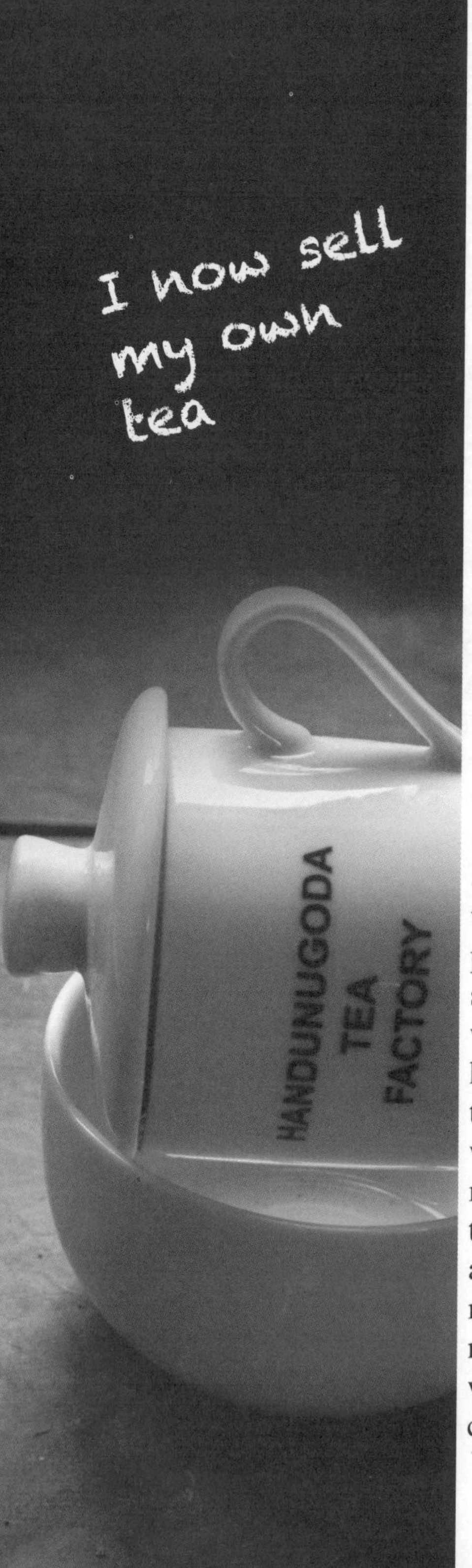

Another incident at the Suicide Club will, I am sure, capture the flavour of the times.

My father, Richard, also joined these sessions at the Suicide Club. He was the District Sales Manager of the Standard Vacuum Oil Company of America. This was a very prestigious position at the time. At one of the sessions of the Suicide Club, when all the wealthy members were participating, my father, too, entered the game. He wiped out the money of all the players with a huge winning spree on that particular day. He had then summoned his driver, Sardiris, and told him to buy a suitcase to carry the money. Having placed his money in the suitcase, he was walking away when another participant, who had lost heavily, mockingly told him, "Richard, you don't walk away after winning so much money. Come, let's finish the game." My father had asked him if he had any more money left on him. "I have no money because you have won it all, but let's play for a cheque, which I will give you if I lose."

My grandfather had told him, 'Richard, when you have won and start walking away from the gambling table, you never return.' Richard Herman Gunaratne disregarded this advice and returned. He lost almost everything that he had won. Chicki Chow was the Chinese professional gambler who had lost. He subsequently recovered a part of his losses. My father, after cleaning out the table, had placed Rs.4000 in his pockets. Other than for this money, he lost all his winnings which were in the suitcase.

Nine hundred acres of Edunkele Estate was thus sold and the debt settled within the stipulated time. Today, I own and live on the acreage that remained after the sale of Edunkele. It was to this plantation that I returned after relinquishing my career.

Kotigala and Edunkele estates were a part of Edunkele. The crops were mainly coconut and rubber. Tea, however, was the passion of my life. By this time the tea plantations had spread into the low lying areas of the Southern Province. I decided to plant the properties with tea. Having done so, I also wanted to build a tea factory. Heavy capital was required to build a tea factory. Capital that I did not have.

I was able to go to the Sampath Bank, where a very old friend, Kumar Abeynaike, was a senior manager. He assisted me to obtain a loan. My knowledge and ability were the collateral. There were many people who assisted me in this project. However, building a tea factory with new machinery was far too costly and the option available to me was to install old machinery. Having worked on the state-owned plantations, I knew exactly where there was surplus equipment.

The Minister of Plantation Industries was General Ranjan Wijeratne, a very senior colleague from the plantations. I met him and told him of my plans. He immediately approved my project and went out of his way to arrange the purchase of the machinery. I dismantled and re-assembled the equipment from Rahanwatte Estate, Lindula. The equipment was transported to Ruhuna under my personal supervision and with the assistance of my two sons.

I thus created my own Plantation Raj, albeit a very modest one.

The whole project was completed in six months. I had to meet the loan instalments on time, however. For this I had to ensure that the tea produced was sold at the best possible price. Running and managing one's own plantation was quite different from managing a plantation for a British company or for the Government of Ceylon. I had to find a vast amount of money at the end of the month to meet the bought leaf payments and to pay my labour. There was no godfather who lodged the money to my bank account. The total amount of tea produced was never sold on time, before the end of the month, but I had to settle the green leaf suppliers on time. This is the biggest problem that a plantation owner faces.

I had to work out a strategy to sell the tea fast and also to obtain the highest price. By this time, I was quite friendly with Mrs. Sirimavo Bandaranaike who was then the Leader of the Opposition and the President of the Sri Lanka Freedom Party. I used to visit her at her ancestral home in Horagolla. She never forgot that I had lost my job because I tried to assist her in developing the handloom industry. I told her of my plans to build a tea factory. She was very keen to assist me in whatever way she could. She told me, "Herman, I am now out of power, but if there is any way I can assist you, please let me know."

Harry Stassen Jayawardena was a very close associate of the Bandaranaikes. He was also the leading tea buyer in the country and one of Ceylon's wealthiest men. I decided to solicit her support to get Harry Jayawardena to look closely at my tea and, if the product satisfied him, to buy the tea. She personally spoke to Harry Jayawardena and wanted me to meet him. The letter that she wrote to me in connection with this is still one of my most prized possessions. I was perhaps the only man in the world to have got a former Prime Minister to assist him in selling his tea!

Letter from Mrs. Bandaranaike

SIRIMAVO R. D. BANDARANAIKE

විපක්ෂ නායක
எதிர்க்கட்சி முதல்வர்
LEADER OF THE OPPOSITION

Parliament,
Sri Jayawardenepura, Kotte.

Telephones
Office 564285, 564253
Residence 694539, 699440

My No. M/C

10th August,1991

Mr M H Gunaratne
Handunugoda Estate
Tittagalla
Ahangama

Dear Mr Guneratne

I am in receipt of your letter 2nd July,1991. The reason for the delay in acknowledging receipt was due to the fact that Mr Harry Jayawardena of Stassens Ltd., was out of the country for over five weeks and returned to Sri Lanka only a short time ago.

In the meantime I was away in upcountry for a week and returned only on a few days ago. Hence the delay in writing. I am sorry about this delay. I have spoken to Mr Harry Jayawardena about your request and he tells me that you have already spoken to him and he is willing to help in whatever way he can.

I have not forgotten how you tried to help me to revive the handloom industry in Attanagalla. After you left I have not got that co-operation from Lanka Fabrics. that I got during your period as Chairman. Things are moving rather stormy and there is not that enthusiasm among the officials. I was sorry that you had to go. Persons who try to do a good job are not appreciated or encouraged. This is just what happened to you.

I wish to take this opportunity to thank you for the co-operation given to me at Attanagalla to revive the handloom industry.

With kind regards

Yours sincerely,

Sirimavo R D Bandaranaike

Sirimavo R D Bandaranaike.

Mrs. Sirimavo Bandaranaike needs very special mention. She was a very charming woman with a lot of old world courtesy and kindness. She went out of her way to support me. She used to speak to me regularly to find out how I was progressing and was genuinely happy at my success. This is quite in contrast with the politicians of today, who simply forget you, once the job is done.

Life in the South was not easy. I had to face the direct wrath of the Janatha Vimukthi Peramuna (JVP) insurrection. This story is written in my book *The Tortured Island.*

I realised later that making tea for the mass market was quite unrewarding and turned my whole manufacturing techniques around to the production of the highest quality speciality teas. Today, teas produced by me on Handunugoda Estate realise the highest price for tea in the world! Some of my teas are sold in the most fashionable tea salons. Mariage Frères in France is considered the temple of tea, situated in Faubourg St. Honoré off the Champs-Élysées. This company markets my Virgin White tea. This is a tea untouched by hand and is said to contain the highest level of antioxidants. I will refrain from telling you the story of the Virgin White as I do not wish to indulge in self aggrandisement. That is not my intention. What is important, however, for the aspiring planting student is to make use of the knowledge that one has gained on the plantations to serve humankind. Virgin White tea is my contribution to the world of tea.

Ceylon is the land of tea. The wealth of our country lies hidden in the lush tea lands spread throughout the length and breadth of our country. The tea industry has passed through many convulsions. Private ownership, state ownership, back again to private ownership and management. The plantations today, however, are in a perilous state and if this situation is not addressed soon, we will lose our pre-eminence in the world of tea.

'*Those who matter do not care. Those who care do not matter.*'

No story on tea would be complete if the contribution made by the Indian plantation worker, by the British planter and the other numerous players in this great human drama, is not told.

My final homage to tea is the Tea Museum that I am developing on Handunugoda. The museum will tell the story of this 150 year-old industry. It will not only consist of antique pieces, but is also billed to capture the magic of tea, the human story behind it and reveal how this great industry came to be the mainstay of the economy of our island home.

History is not only about old machines and antiquities. It is the story of man, land and water, of great human enterprise, passion, disappointments, struggles and devotion to duty. It is the human story of tea that I will depict in my museum. It will be my final homage to tea, the most noble beverage in the world. I will then ride happily into the sunset.

Sunset and evening star,
And one last call for me!
And may there be no moaning at the bar
When I put out to sea.

Alfred, Lord Tennyson

The end.

SUPERINTENDENT's
BUNGALOW
CIRCUIT
BUNGALOW